Jerry Green

OF THE TIGER

Detroit's World Champions

Coward-McCann, Inc.   **New York**

To Mom, *who made the sandwiches and packed the brown paper bags and listened to the endless talk and never quite comprehended the appeal of the ball games; and to Nancy, my wife, who assumed the burden after the peanut-butter-and-jelly era and who even attended a game in the Year of the Tiger.*

ACKNOWLEDGMENTS

Mrs. Yvonne Warren, secretary to the sports department of the Detroit *News*, for her manuscript typing and author prodding.

The gentlemen of the Detroit Chapter of the Baseball Writers Association—Watson Spoelstra, chapter chairman and national president.

The gentlemen of the Detroit Baseball Company who communicated.

INTRODUCTION

We won.

After sixteen years in the big leagues, I was in the World Series. It was an incredible year. No ball club before us ever had one like it.

It was the year Denny McLain was striving to become the first pitcher in the lifetimes of most of us on the Tigers to win 30 games in a season.

It was the year when game after game one of us would get a hit in the ninth inning to win a game we could not lose. That was our style.

It was the year our manager, Mayo Smith, made adjustments, maneuvered players, sometimes gambled, sometimes followed the regular managerial doctrine. Almost everything he attempted worked.

It was the year we played in the World Series, and even there won our championship in our own fashion.

It was an amazing and wonderful year.

And during most of our year, there was a vacuum. Detroit's two newspapers were closed by a strike until August. Many of our accomplishments were unrecorded.

We would sit in our clubhouse after ball games and watch Jerry Green frantically scribbling in his notebook. We'd wonder what he would do with all his notes.

Here is the answer, his diary of the Year of the Tiger. I am glad, after all, there is a permanent record of our year.

Franklin, Michigan   AL KALINE
December 17, 1968

YEAR OF THE TIGER

Al Kaline had to wonder whether he'd ever play in a World Series.

Malcolm W. Emmons

PROLOGUE—OCTOBER 1, 1967

They were baseball fans, people. They came, alone or in twos, hurdling the fences. They scampered around the outfield, toward the athletes, chased by out-of-condition ushers wearing Kelly green uniforms. Then Dick McAuliffe grounded into a double play. It was over. The Detroit Tigers had lost the pennant again. They had done this for twenty-two years. They hadn't won since Captain Hank Greenberg had come back from World War II in 1945. But this year it had been closer than the others.

The people came now in multitudes, people turned into an uncontrolled crowd in a city already violated by riot this same summer. This was different. There were blacks and whites in this throng, bound by something common—failure of a baseball team. It was frustration, the human response to being tantalized by victory and then, again, defeat.

This mob attacked the cement dugouts and tore the leather mats from the wooden benches. They smashed the water coolers, ripped the piping. They picked up the rusting metal box seats and hurled them over the fences onto the ball field. They invaded the pitcher's mound and dug away with penknives at the rubber slab anchored in the dirt. Ushers fought fans with their fists. An usher was dropped to the seat of his green trousers right on the mound.

The police came. The baseball season was over, and in three days, in Boston, that improbable city, the World Series would begin.

Inside, in a dank runway to the clubhouse, a ballplayer fired a baseball at a television cameraman. He missed and tried again and scored.

Mayo Smith, the manager, a man with a hawkish, sun-lined face, attempted to explain what had gone wrong. He then tried to say what would go right in 1968. In baseball there is always next year.

"Of course, I've got plans," said Smith, who had been fired at Philadelphia and Cincinnati because his ballplayers were ordinary.

Smith used eight pitchers in this final game against California, trying to save the Tigers from elimination. All year he had tried to find a dependable relief pitcher, and when he found one, he overworked the arm.

"I'm a gambler and I ride a hot horse," said Smith, the manager, who really could not be considered a gambler. Rather the sportswriters covering the team regarded Smith as a bland man without imagination—just another conservative baseball manager.

Smith had not started this game, this last one the Tigers had to win to tie for the American League pennant, with a hot horse. He started the game with the only rested arm he had on his pitching staff.

It belonged to a young, brash man named Dennis McLain, a 20-game winner the previous year. But this summer Denny McLain had been merely a good pitcher with 17 victories. He did not win a game in the entire month of September as four bunched teams cascaded for a pennant only one could win

McLain had not pitched for two weeks. His previous start was against the Red Sox in a critical game at Tiger Stadium. McLain was knocked out in the third inning—and here there are varying accounts of what occurred.

One version—the accepted one as related by McLain—was that he went home and fell asleep on his sofa while watching television. Later there was some rattling at the garbage pails outside the garage, and McLain said he awoke startled. His leg was all pins and needles. It gave way as McLain started off to investigate the noise in the night.

The result was several dislocated toes.

Other versions mentioned a kicked-in water fountain in the Tigers' clubhouse.

McLain was knocked out in the third inning of the final game. It was then that Smith started his procession of relief pitchers in an effort to win the game.

One of the pitchers was Mickey Lolich, a floppy-eared, potbellied left-hander. Lolich was born a right-hander but became left-handed after a motorcycle fell atop him as a toddler in Portland, Oregon. During the season, he had lost 10 games in a row. But toward the end Lolich was the Tigers' most reliable pitcher.

He had pitched a shutout yesterday over the Angels to keep the Tigers in the pennant race. But they had lost the second game of a doubleheader by squandering a four-run lead, damaged by a pitcher throwing to the wrong base.

Then again on this final day, the Tigers won their first game and had to win their second. They had a 3–1 lead behind McLain but were unable to hold it. Smith beckoned to six pitchers after McLain and then Lolich finally. It was 8–5 favor the Angels in the ninth.

A rally was needed in the ninth, a last-inning uprising—the game isn't over till the last man is out. Bill Freehan doubled and Don Wert walked and there was a chance. But Jim Price flied out. And then McAuliffe hit the grounder to second base. A double play and it was all over, again, twenty-two straight years without a pennant.

The Tigers were not a team with flair. They were not a team possessed, like the Red Sox, with the ability to achieve the melodramatic, to win with a stirring comeback in the final inning.

In the clubhouse Al Kaline, the team's veteran star, slumped on a stool in front of his double locker in the corner. His fifteenth season in the big leagues was over. Al Kaline, batting champion at twenty, was going to miss the World Series for the fifteenth time. No, he wouldn't bother traveling to Boston and St. Louis. He had never wished to do a World Series that way. Why battle the crowds and sit in the grandstands? No, he had never seen a World Series game, except on television and even then with disinterest. Yes, there was some envy for those lucky enough to play in a World Series.

"Look, I think the fact that I haven't played in the World Series has been greatly overplayed," said Kaline. "I'd certainly love to be in the World Series, but I'm certainly not going to go into an insane asylum if I don't play in one. It's not an obsession with me."

In June, before the pennant race had become hysteria, Kaline had struck out against Cleveland's Sam McDowell. The Tigers had not been playing well and were being easily defeated this night. Kaline had been a moody young player. But he had matured and performed so coolly he sometimes was criticized for indifference.

After McDowell struck him out, Kaline walked back to the dugout, holding the uncooperative bat. Once inside, enraged, he slammed the bat into its rack. He slammed his little finger against the rack in the same impulsive act.

"You'd better look at my hand," Kaline told trainer Bill Behm a few moments later. "I think I've broken something."

Kaline missed more than a month while the broken bone mended. He was humiliated and blamed himself for the dumbest thing he'd ever done. But he returned to help the Tigers in August and September.

"I know the players felt we had the best team and should have won the pennant," Kaline said when the race ended with the loss to the Angels.

"One game doesn't mean that much. We had a hundred and sixty-two games to do it and we didn't. It's been a tremendous experience for the guys on this team who'll be back next year."

McLain, Kaline—bizarre injuries . . . Eddie Mathews, an accidental flight downstairs, headfirst, at home . . . Jim Northrup out with the mumps . . . Willie Horton playing on an intensely painful heel . . . Mayo Smith himself pulling a hamstring muscle running to the outfield when Horton hurt himself.

"Detroit should win the pennant by ten games," agitated Eddie Stanky, the mouthy manager of the Chicago White Sox, back while the four-team race was boiling.

But in Boston, the 100–1 shot Red Sox listened to the piped-in broadcast of the Tigers' final game. When McAuliffe grounded into the double play, the most dramatic pennant race in history was ended.

Carl Yastrzemski sprayed champagne and spoke boastfully with a hoarse voice about the Red Sox into the network microphone.

And Tiger Stadium, once the maintenance men cleansed it, would now belong to the Detroit Lions for the pro football season. Bill Freehan, the catcher, would go out and sit alone in the grandstand behind first base and watch the football players at practice. This was better than listening to the World Series from Boston.

"It will hurt forever," said Freehan.

APRIL 9, 1968

Forever!

The printed schedules called today the opening day of the 1968 baseball season. But Dr. Martin Luther King is dead, assassinated, and baseball season can wait.

The Tigers worked out at their ball park, the opening day bunting draped, but no people. Earl Wilson was an hour late.

Wilson, 22-game winner and manager Smith's opening day selection, was grim, seemingly bitter. Only a black man could feel the deepest anguish over Dr. King's murder.

Mayo Smith, the gambling nongambler, had a surprise.

"Mickey Stanley is playing first base tomorrow," said Smith. "Boston is pitching a left-hander and we want as many right-handed batters as we can get."

So Stanley, who excels in center field with a finger glove, took throws in infield practice at first with a borrowed first baseman's mitt.

"Look at our pitching staff," said Smith.

Only the four starters remained from the 13-man staff the Tigers had a year ago today. The bullpen, where the Tigers failed in 1967, was entirely different.

Smith, indeed, was gambling on young arms, inexperienced but strong, to rescue his starters. The relief corps averaged twenty-four years of age. Smith had the same starters—Wilson, Lolich, Joe Sparma and McLain.

McLain—the pitcher Smith deemed most expendable during the off-season. He had almost been traded to Baltimore in a three-way deal with the Yankees. But the Orioles had backed off.

Now, on this gray day, McLain looked different. His hair was no longer dirty blond, cut short. Instead, red hair, a gaudy color red, strung out from beneath the cap McLain wore on a high perch, obscuring his forehead.

It was still the same old Denny.

Out in Las Vegas, citadel of top nightclub entertainment and the bookmakers, the Tigers were favorites to win the pennant.

APRIL 10—OPENING DAY

Booooo. . . .

Welcome back, Mayo Smith. The Tigers were greeted by their largest opening day crowd in seven years, despite th postponement and the cold. The assemblage was more than 41,000 even though Governor Romney's curfew, enforced since the assassination, was modified just four hours before he threw the traditional first pitch into the dirt.

The Tigers hit the bright lights, all over town.

THE YEAR OF THE TIGER. The proclamation was flashed from the gas company sign to motorists bumper to bumper on the expressway going downtown. The same prediction was delivered from the lighted bulb sign atop the Chrysler plant out on the east side.

Year of the Tiger, nonsense.

The Red Sox won opening day, 7–3. Earl Wilson hit a homer, but he was driven out of the game in the sixth inning.

Mickey Stanley misplayed a couple of grounders at first base. Norm Cash cringed on the bench.

Cash, who once batted .361, had watched the Tigers lose the pennant the previous October from the same seat. Unable to make a trade for a new first baseman, the Tigers kept him. But against a left-handed pitcher, Mayo Smith was dictated to by percentages and kept Cash on the bench.

"I had a good spring," dissented Cash, a left-handed swinger who always had been troubled by left-handed pitching. "I hit left-handers.

"I'm surprised I'm not playing. There's no excuse for it."

Ray Oyler was the shortstop. He hit .207 last year, and the Tigers actively sought to trade for another shortstop during the winter. They almost had Luis Aparicio from Baltimore in a deal that would have included McLain. But it didn't work out.

Dick Ellsworth, Boston's pitcher, struck out Oyler the first two at-bats. In the seventh, with the Tigers floundering, 6–1, Oyler fouled a ball toward third base. The crowd cheered mightily, in derision. He fouled off three more pitches and the crowd cheered each.

In the eighth, there were two baserunning mistakes. Then Willie Horton doubled to left and Yastrzemski made the misjudgment of throwing behind him to second, which nobody covered. Horton lighted for third, chased by George Scott, the first baseman.

It so happened that Al Kaline already occupied third. Scott touched the ball to Horton and he was declared out.

"This is the first game of the season," Mayo Smith rationalized. "We lost the first game last year. Twinkletoes Horton got his head down. It's good to see Willie running on that foot anyway."

Willie Horton's surgical heel was the major concern of spring training. He'd limped through it, sometimes in agony, sometimes resting.

"Stanley disappointed me in the field," said Smith of his first experiment of the year. "But he had three hits.

"I'll find a place for him."

And you wondered just how Mayo Smith would find places for four very good outfielders at the same time.

How could he play Kaline, Horton, Stanley and Jim Northrup? And how could he manage to play without one of them?

APRIL 11

Gates Brown is available—via trade or cash.

"I'd like another right-handed pinch hitter," said Mayo Smith. "We have plenty of left-handers."

The Tigers started trying to dispose of Brown, their number three left-handed pinch hitter, when they returned from the South. But there was no interest. No team wanted Brown in trade or for cash or even as a gift.

So on the second afternoon of the new season he sat on the bench in the Tigers' dugout and watched.

He watched as Denny McLain, the redhead, made his first

pitching start of the year. Under Smith's rotation plans, it was Mickey Lolich's turn to start because he was number two on the staff. But Lolich was still on duty with the Air National Guard motor pool on the 7 A.M. to 3 P.M. tour. Lolich had been called up following Dr. King's assassination. After duty on opening day, he rushed to the ball park and warmed up in the late innings in the bullpen.

But he was unable to start today, and Smith worked McLain instead. Denny did all right against the Red Sox with a 3–0 lead into the sixth. But then the home run pitch returned. It always had been a problem for McLain, even when he was good. Joe Lahoud, a teen-age Red Sox rookie, socked a two-run homer and Rico Petrocelli followed with another homer and McLain was tied up.

Smith pinch-hit for him in the seventh, and Eddie Mathews, the first left-handed pinch hitter, walked. The Tigers loaded the bases with one out—but they couldn't get a run across to permit McLain to leave as the potential winner.

Brown watched from his seat as Jon Warden, one of the new relief pitchers, faced the Red Sox in the eighth. Last year while Yastrzemski was leading the league in everything, Warden was pitching in the deep minors at Rocky Mount, North Carolina.

Warden got out of a bases-loaded situation in the eighth as Smith had unusual patience with a relief pitcher.

In the ninth he retired the first two batters, and the third batter was Yaz, who had hit two homers opening day.

Bill Freehan, the catcher, walked to the mound.

"Keep the ball down," he said.

Warden struck Yaz out with a pitch at eye level.

Tom Matchick, the number two left-handed pinch hitter, was used in the eighth. Smith had only Brown left to bat for Warden leading off the ninth.

Brown cracked the pitch by John Wyatt deep into the upper grandstand in right field. The Tigers were winners, 4–3, for the first time in the new season on a last licks run.

At home plate the Tigers, accused of lacking enthusiasm during 1967's failure, mobbed unwanted Gates Brown.

"That was my first home run since I hit one in the second game last year, too," said Gates Brown.

Brown always had some sort of special knack against Boston—ever since he hit a homer against the Red Sox in his first big league at-bat.

"I knew he isn't superhuman," said rookie Jon Warden about his confrontation with the Great Yaz. "The pitch wasn't where I wanted it. I released the ball a little high. It was a bad slider. Oh, it was a good one. It didn't do what I wanted it to do."

APRIL 14

For once the tireless Mr. Eddie Stanky was silenced

His great experiment this year with the White Sox was the employment of Pete Ward as his right fielder.

The Tigers beat the White Sox yesterday when Mickey Stanley's normal fly ball to right was misjudged by Ward Two runs tramped in to break a 1–1 tie for the Tigers victory.

Today Stanky had Ward back at his old position, third base, and the Tigers and White Sox went into the tenth with the score tied.

Now in the tenth, Dick McAuliffe singled, leading off. The obvious strategy was for Kaline to bunt Mac up to second Stanky, the percentage man, expected a bunt, and Mayo Smith considered it. But then Smith had a thought. Kaline swung away and hit a single and Mac went to third.

Stanky would take care of that. He brought in Hoyt Wil

helm, the forty-five-year-old knuckle ball expert. Wilhelm walked Horton on purpose to load the bases, the percentage move. Then he knuckled two strikes over on Bill Freehan.

Freehan knuckled the next pitch back toward Pete Ward at third base. The grounder scratched off his glove and McAuliffe scored the winning run in Last Licks Victory Number Two. Freehan was rewarded with a single, and Eddie Stanky had no comment.

Mayo Smith's bullpen had its third straight victory. Fred Lasher, a submarine pitcher who developed his underarm motion scaling rocks across the surface of a lake, was the relief winner.

Lasher had been brought up late last year and was Smith's last-gasp relief hope in the stretch. Through his September burden he now had the most experience of the five young arms in the bullpen.

"At least they can throw the ball past hitters and get strikeouts," said Smith. "Last year's relief pitchers always needed pinpoint control. When they didn't have it, they got hit, hit hard.

"I don't want to go through that again this year."

APRIL 17

"We're winning the games we didn't win last year," Mayo Smith decided sometime this afternoon.

The Tigers had returned home from a one-game visit to Boston, where the Red Sox had hoisted their 1967 pennant. The Tigers responded with a 15-hit battering, an 8-run rally and an easy 9–2 victory for Earl Wilson. It was the Tigers' fourth straight, and Wilson was the first starter to win a game.

Earl Wilson

Malcolm W. Emmons

Now it was a sullen Wednesday afternoon, made more gloomy by Sam McDowell's fastball. The ball jumped at the Tigers through the grayness and they couldn't touch it.

In the first inning McDowell struck out Kaline in their first meeting since last June. Kaline again walked slowly back to the dugout but was more cautious about replacing his bat.

Two years ago Denny McLain and McDowell had a brief but wordy feud.

"I want to beat him so bad I can taste it," McLain told a Detroit baseball writer before a matchup.

They were the two best young pitchers in the league, both strong-armed, brashly confident and garrulous. One night they exchanged notes from clubhouse to clubhouse via messenger in Cleveland. They were not friendly notes.

When their rivalry finally reached the pitching mound after considerable buildup in the public prints, neither survived through the third inning.

Again today they opposed each other, and this time each pitched magnificently. McLain, making his second start, dropped one run behind and had to leave for a pinch hitter after seven innings.

The Indians and McDowell hugged a 2–1 lead into the bottom of the ninth. Then Freehan led off with a single to center. The situation was similar to the one the other day; a bunt was the conventional strategy. This time Smith did have Don Wert bunt and Freehan was sacrificed to second.

McDowell struck out Northrup and the Tigers were one out away from the end of their winning streak. Smith sent Jimmy Price up to pinch-hit for Oyler.

Two curve ball strikes put McDowell one pitch from victory. Price hit that pitch, a fastball, into center field, and Freehan scored the tying run.

Another late-inning rally . . . but the Indians scored themselves in the top of the tenth. It was getting darker, and Eddie Fisher, a knuckleballer, relieved for the Indians in the bottom of the inning.

He got the first two outs on simple fly balls. Again the Indians were an out away from snapping the Tigers' streak.

Fisher walked Kaline. The next batter was Willie Horton, a power swinger going up against a fluttery knuckle ball. Wally Moses, the batting tutor, often preached to Horton that a soft stroke was needed to catch the knuckler.

"I'm going to try to hit it to right field," Horton told Smith.

Smith nodded approval.

"I want to get Al over to third," Horton continued.

Fisher quickly got two knuckling strikes on him, and again the Tigers were a pitch away from the end of the winning streak.

Just meet it, hit it to right or center, don't try to pull it, Horton remembered the advice from Moses.

Horton just met the next knuckle ball, and the ball traveled on a line over the left-field fence, low.

At second base, unemotional Al Kaline started dancing and swinging his arms in two circles, round and round. When he reached second base, Horton recalled later, he realized he had hit a home run.

The final score was 4–3, Last Licks Victory Number Three, and at home plate there was a mass celebration for Willie Horton.

"That was my best knuckler—no other right-handed batter has ever hit my knuckler like that before," said Fisher, who had been a big leaguer since 1961.

The Tigers went to the clubhouse believing they were destined to win the pennant. They were 5–1, but not yet in first place, for the Minnesota Twins were 6–0.

"Minnesota wins again today," said Jim Northrup to Al Kaline. "We're still behind them, but they haven't beaten any good teams. All they've played is Washington and New York. Washington had the best spring training record."

"Yeah, and Minnesota had the worst," said Kaline. "It shows how much spring training means."

"How much does all this mean now?" said Mayo Smith. "It's very, very early. We'll win some more like this—and lose some, too."

"I made up my mind to stay down and go to right field," apologized game-winner Horton. "It was a good knuckle ball, down and out. Really, I wasn't trying to pull it."

It was the fourth victory in five games from the new bullpen. Young Jon Warden had won for the second time, pitching to one batter . . . and, my, wasn't the big leagues something easy!

APRIL 18

As a youth in Baltimore, Al Kaline had often played for four sandlot teams in the same day. His uncle would drive him from one field to the other. Kaline would change his uniforms in the back seat while his uncle drove.

When Al was eighteen, Ed Katalinas, the Tigers' chief scout, offered him a contract for $35,000. Kaline signed it. Under the rules in 1953, bonus players had to remain on the big league roster. So in June that year Kaline, a skinny teenager, joined the Tigers. He hit a pinch-hit fly ball to center fielder Ed McGhee in his first big league at-bat in Philadelphia.

Al Kaline played in his two thousandth major league game today.

"I wish I would start hitting," he said before the game. "I'm taking strikes and swinging at balls."

The Indians' Steve Hargan struck him out the first two times up. Then in the fifth, Kaline connected and hit a wrong-field homer to right. It was the 305th of his career, one below Hank Greenberg's Detroit club record.

"You can't expect to play with one club so long," Al Kaline said in his corner of the clubhouse. "Especially when you're with so many losers. You expect the club to make changes. I wish I didn't know about it. I'm starting to feel old. Two more home runs for the record. I hope I can completely blank my mind of that."

Joe Sparma pitched a shutout and the 5–0 victory increased the Tigers' winning streak to six. They had moved into first place in a tie with the Twins. Washington broke Minnesota's winning streak by picking Rod Carew off third base with the bases loaded in the ninth.

"I had veal scallopini for breakfast today," said Joe Sparma, offering that as a breakfast of champions. "Usually I have sausage and peppers, but today it was veal scallopini."

APRIL 21

The Tigers flew to Chicago with a 6–1 record. Eddie Stanky's White Sox, a supposed pennant contender, were 0–6.

"The biggest thing is to win each series," said Mayo Smith, the new sage. "Two out of three, three out of four, split a few. That's the way I'd like it."

He then was ominous.

"Streaks are followed by other streaks."

The Tigers had won six straight; the White Sox had lost six.

Smith firmly believed the law of averages was part of baseball's constitution. Thirteen years before, he had managed the Phillies. He suffered with them through a 13-game losing streak. Then they won a game, and another, and another—until they had won 11 in a row.

Yesterday the Tigers had failed to bunt four times and could not get Mickey Lolich a run until the ninth. But the bullpen gave it back, and in the tenth the Tigers won their third extra-inning game of the week, 4–1.

It was Last Licks Victory Number Four, and the Tigers were all alone in first place when the Yankees beat the Twins.

Jon Warden, the rookie from Rocky Mount, this time faced two batters and won his third game in his third big league appearance.

Today Denny McLain, winless in his first two starts, won his first game, 4–2. It was in the second game of a double-header after Earl Wilson won the opener, 4–1. The bullpen rested.

Pete Ward contributed again. He booted a grounder in the second inning of the opener. The Tigers flooded across all four of their runs, all unearned.

In the second game Ward bobbled a grounder by Oyler, and McLain followed by driving in the first run. Ward later fumbled a double-play grounder and the Tigers scored two more runs.

For the day, the Tigers scored eight times, and six of the runs were unearned. The White Sox scored three runs, all driven in on Ward's two home runs.

McLain missed a shutout in the ninth on Ward's homer.

The two streaks endured the series—the Tigers leaving with nine successive victories, Stanky's White Sox without a victory after nine games.

The last-place White Sox trailed the league-leading Tigers ten days into the season by eight and a half games. Good-bye, Eddie, thanks, and see you in June.

APRIL 24

Most of the Tigers' achievements belong to history, back two decades or before. Hal Middlesworth, the club's public relations specialist, had to dig deeply into the archives to establish the previous winning streak of this magnitude.

The Tigers had not won nine straight games since 1949, when Al Kaline was fourteen and Denny McLain a prekindergartener in Chicago.

Despite the nine victories, the Tigers had hit the ball well in only one game. Timely hits and opponents' errors and pinch hitters and relief pitchers put the Tigers into first place.

Mayo Smith considered the Tigers a team of hitters, power hitters. To him the winning streak was so marvelous because the Tigers were winning with nonhitting. Eventually they would hit, he knew.

"Now we're taking instead of giving," Smith declared as the Tigers moved into Cleveland. "You don't beat anybody in this game; you can capitalize on the mistakes of the other teams and let them beat themselves.

"We've been getting the breaks. To get the kind we have is what it takes to win the pennant."

The Tigers, through their years of midsummer frustration, had won many pennants in January and in March. The very word—*pennant*—was eliminated from their conversation, almost annually, in April. Now Mayo Smith had used it in April. He had outlined the way a team can win a pennant.

"This team is better because it believes in itself now," said Smith. "It took a while to accomplish that."

The Tigers had been awed, bemused, last summer and fall by their mere presence in a pennant race.

Now the season was two weeks old, and the Tigers had won nine of ten games, .900.

"The objective of the first two weeks," said Mayo Smith, "was to stay above .500, somehow."

"We have a new approach," said Bill Freehan. "Last year we always thought today maybe we can win. If we didn't, we thought we'll try to win tomorrow. This year there is no maybe. The pennant is right there—ours to take. We think only about winning today."

Tonight they would not hit much again. It was a shivery

night, a strong wind swirled on the Lake Erie shoreline, and it was only 36 degrees. It wasn't much of a night for the hitters; their hands stung even through the golf gloves.

Through seven runless innings Steve Hargan dueled with Joe Sparma. Hargan granted the Tigers one hit, by Northrup. He faced the minimum number of 21 batters.

In the bottom of the seventh there was a throwing error by McAuliffe at second. Hargan then popped a fly into shallow left. Ray Oyler drifted back from shortstop. Horton stepped in from left field.

It was quiet in the near-empty Cleveland Stadium, except for the howl of the chill wind. Oyler gloved the ball, but crushingly Horton slammed into him. The ball dropped and fell onto the grass. A run scored and Hargan reached third with a fluke triple.

Oyler, outweighed by 30 pounds, arose quickly. But Willie Horton, the slugger, was unconscious. He was taken from the field on a stretcher, and examination showed he had a concussion.

Hargan scored from third when the game resumed.

The final score was Cleveland 2, Detroit 0—and the Tigers had only that one hit by Northrup.

The winning streak was ended—but the lead was two games over the Twins.

APRIL 28

One of Mayo Smith's pleasures is his daily visit to the pressroom. He loves to stand at a corner of the bar with a postgame drink and socialize with the baseball writers. There is conversation, good talk about baseball and plenty of agitation.

Two of the many faces of manager Mayo Smith.

Mayo likes it, and he will screw up his hawkish face and make himself look like a grinning gargoyle. He does this whenever he is jabbed with a statement of agitating sarcasm or a deliberately silly question designed to annoy. A question such as: "Why don't you change the script and score some runs early because this bit of winning games in the last inning is becoming overworked, you know?"

And Mayo will stamp his foot on the floor and squint up that face of his and say, "Oh, you bastard, you," or something. Then he'll laugh and the writers will laugh with him.

First place was fun, even in the insecurity of the very early season.

Mayo particularly likes to visit Yankee Stadium in New York. There is a well-appointed pressroom and plenty of writers. Smith knows them well from his days as a superscout employed by the Yankees.

The regular Detroit writers, Watson Spoelstra of the *News* and George Cantor of the *Free Press*, weren't along on this trip. Detroit was suffering through one of its periodic newspaper strikes. So the writers had to stay home and grieve.

"If the papers stay on strike all year, the Tigers can win the pennant," said Billy Hoeft, an old left-hander, on a TV pregame show.

But the Tigers' organization and sensible people scoffed at that assertion. They remembered how little help Hoeft had been toward a pennant when he pitched for Detroit.

So Mayo Smith took his first-place ball club into the baseball showplace, the media and communications capital.

And here for their premiere before the New York press the first-place Tigers, so magnificent a few days ago, were in a terrible slump.

They played poorly, looked bad the first night in New York for a four-game weekend series. This was the night the impressions would be created.

The Yankees' Mel Stottlemyre handled the Tigers on three hits and held them without a run, 5–0. The Tigers, thus, had accumulated four hits and no runs in their two games since the winning streak.

But not only did they fail to hit. They were embarrassed. A Yankee stole a base in each of the first three innings. They perpetrated a double steal in the sixth. In all, the Yankees stole five bases in the game.

The bullpen had done well—but the starters' results did not match the great expectations. Wilson, the ace, had pitched well twice and won, and also lost twice. Sparma had pitched well in two of three starts, but had a 1–1 record. Lolich was 0–0 and back in the National Guard for the weekend. McLain was 1–0 in three strong performances. Twice he had been removed for pinch hitters and the Tigers had won in later innings, as was becoming their fashion.

Now, next day, it was McLain's assignment to stop what could become a tailspin, remembering Smith's statement about streaks begetting reverse streaks.

McLain's second victory of the season was a five-hit shut-out, 7–0. He had not pitched this well since before he damaged himself last September and became useless during the Tigers' abortive pennant run.

Jim Northrup started to hit against the Yankees. He homered and had two other hits. McAuliffe singled in two runs and later hit a homer.

Home runs were becoming the Tigers' primary weapon, despite the early-season coolness and the edge the pitchers had on the hitters in April. Already, throughout baseball, it seemed 1968 would be a year for the pitchers.

With their two home runs, the Tigers equaled their entire production for last year in Yankee Stadium—home of the home run.

Danger—perpetuation of the losing streak following the winning streak—had been averted before today's doubleheader.

Joe Sparma pitched the first game and had a no-hitter until the seventh. Then he lost the game in the eighth when Mickey Mantle broke a 0–0 tie with a double off Warden.

Les Cain, another of the new arms, made his first major league appearance in the second game, with Lolich in the Guard for the weekend. Cain was a prodigy, just twenty, up from a losing year at Montgomery.

The Tigers considered him the best young pitcher in their farm system. Everything he did against the Yankees supported their vision.

The second scoreless duel of the afternoon again went into the seventh when the Tigers scored on Don Wert's single. But in the eighth Cain was touched for a tying homer by Andy Kosco, a nearly forgotten Tiger prodigy of another time. Kosco, who had drifted around the minors with brief appearances in the majors, had smacked only the twentieth ball into Yankee Stadium's deep left-field bleachers.

Smith decided to remove Cain. The Yankees promptly went ahead with another run. Pat Dobson walked a man, threw two wild pitches and permitted a single. John Hiller came in and retired the Yankees, who had runners on first and third with none out.

So the Tigers, fortunately, went into the ninth trailing only 2–1. Freehan hit a home run, Northrup hit a home run, and the Tigers won, 3–2. It was Last Licks Victory Number Five.

After his home run Northrup went out to left field and glared at the customers seated in the stands. Throughout the doubleheader they pelted him with oranges and apples and cherry bombs. Once a rubber ball with steel wires impaled into it whizzed toward him, but it missed.

"One guy hit me with his lunch," said Northrup, a man with some temper. "Once I turned around and told them I'd knock their ———— heads off, and that really set them off.

"We used to have fun at games when we were kids, but my dad would have broken my neck if I'd done stuff like that."

His game-winning homer was an effective silencer.

So the Tigers flew home to Detroit with an 11–4 record and a two-game lead over the Orioles, Twins and Senators.

APRIL 29

Bill Freehan has a ritual when he is struck by an errant pitch in the left elbow or the back or somewhere. It happens frequently, last year on twenty painful occasions.

Freehan will grimace his moon face in a display of agony and teeth. Some words will flow through his lips and he'll glare at the umpire. Finally, he'll depart for first base in that weaving football player's trot. At first base he'll rub the injured area and be thankful he did not follow his initial impulse to rush the pitcher.

Mickey Lolich pitched tonight, and the game with the Oakland A's was another close one. It was 1–0 Tigers entering the ninth, but the A's tied it.

Freehan led off the bottom of the ninth and toppled into the dirt.

"Take your base," said Bill Haller, the plate ump.

Freehan weaved his trot down to first. Norm Cash forced him and advanced to second on a walk. With two outs, Wert lined a single sharply to center field, where Rick Monday had just been installed because of his arm.

Cash barreled around third, and Monday's throw was 15 feet ahead of him in Rene Lachemann's catcher's mitt. It was an easy out. But the pounding feet, perhaps, frightened the ball from the glove, and Cash cracked into the catcher. Lachemann was prone at the plate and Cash stepped over him to score the winning run.

It was Last Licks Victory Number Six, 2–1, credited to Freehan's undesirable habit of being hit by pitched balls.

"To tell you the truth, it didn't hit me," said Freehan a few minutes later. "That's the first time that's happened to me. I'm just getting even."

A smile split the round face.

"Hey, that was the winning run," said Freehan. "Don't say anything about it."

Mickey Lolich was the last of the four starting pitchers to win. He does not resemble an athlete very much with his bulging belly, large ears and sense of humor. Then again, he doesn't remind many people of a soldier, either.

Because of his Guard duty, Lolich was away from the Tigers for more than a week. Such inactivity could have required a refresher trip to spring training.

If there had been a tenth inning tonight, Mayo Smith would have again been forced to call to his bullpen. Lolich yielded only four hits in the nine innings, but now he was exhausted. He waited in the dugout to see what the batters could do in the bottom of the ninth. They won for him, using their bodies more than their hitting.

"I just sat down and became a fan in the ninth," Lolich said. "I hadn't pitched in nine days.

"Oh, I threw in that time. The other day I called the coach at Romeo High School near my house and asked if I could pitch to his players. He said okay, so I went out and threw against them for forty minutes.

"The kids racked me. I was keeping them over the plate and the kids kept popping them over the fence. It's about two hundred seventy down the line.

"All those kids must have gone home and told their fathers they were hitting home runs off a major league pitcher."

MAY 1

"What about it, Denny?" wondered a whimsical Minneapolis baseball writer. "Would you like to earn a hundred thousand dollars next year?"

It was meant as a joke. McLain, who has a passion for money, treated the question that way.

"I made some pitches to Oliva that if I pitch that way all the time will let me go in and ask for a million dollars next year."

Tony Oliva twice had been the American League's batting champion. Tonight McLain handled him with simplicity, almost disdain. He retired Oliva four straight times. The first three times McLain struck him out.

The Twins were in town for the first series between the two clubs now regarded as the chief pennant contenders. The

Whether or not he dyed his hair wasn't nearly as important as the fact Denny McLain was unbeaten.

Camera 5 (Lester Sloan)

Tigers were surviving solely on their pitching. The composite staff earned-run average was 2.18, excellent. In contrast, the team batting average was almost the same, .224, miserable. Even Ray Oyler's batting average was above Jim Northrup's, Al Kaline's, Dick McAuliffe's and Norm Cash's.

The pitchers were being supported with barely enough runs to win. Like tonight. McLain beat the Twins, 3–2, for his third straight victory over the full distance. He was still unbeaten and his hair was still red. Watson Spoelstra of the silenced *News* wrote a story for *Sporting News* about McLain's dyeing his hair.

McLain vociferously denied that he dyed his hair.

In the eighth inning the score was tied, 2–2. The Tigers' two came on Northrup's homer. Then with one out, McAuliffe lined to left field, where Rich Reese, a first baseman in foreign territory, misplayed it into a triple. Willie Horton drove in the winning run with a sacrifice fly ball.

It was Last Licks Victory Number Seven—seven of the Tigers' thirteen victories had been resolved in this fashion. The Tigers had won six of their seven one-run decisions.

"You've got to get pitching for that," said Mayo Smith. "We're not hitting."

"This is the worst hitting slump I've ever seen this club in," said general manager Jim Campbell.

The Twins' two runs were scored on home runs by Harmon Killebrew and Reese. McLain always had been troubled by his generosity to home run hitters and by mere slap hitters suddenly strengthened in Tiger Stadium. The Detroit park is a paradise for the hitters. This was part of McLain's trouble. Once he had considered opening a restaurant as a sideline.

"I'll call it the Upper Deck," he said.

Tonight he talked about Tiger Stadium again and its contours.

"As far as I'm concerned, they can take this park and throw it into the Atlantic Ocean," he said.

MAY 2

Mayo Smith, the clairvoyant, had said the Tigers would—some day—lose the way they had been winning.

Tonight his prophecy was realized. Tonight Al Salerno became an untouchable. Tonight the Tigers lost to the Twins, 3–2, in the last inning, the tenth, by one run.

The magic wore off tonight.

In the bottom of the tenth inning, after the Twins scored, the Tigers loaded the bases. This was their way of winning. Already in the ninth, losing 2–1, Northrup had homered to send the game into the extra inning.

But with the bases loaded in the tenth, Al Worthington struck out Bill Freehan and then Dick Tracewski. It was Last Licks Loss Number One.

Until 2:15 in the morning, upstairs in the front office refreshment room, Mayo Smith kept cussing about Al Salerno.

Salerno was the home plate umpire. In the sixth Salerno called Eddie Mathews out on strikes and then ejected him from the game for complaining.

From then on, Salerno and the customers seated behind the screen near home plate were bickering. The people yelled and threw things and Salerno glared. Once he walked to the stands and picked up a wayward scorebook and flung it at a patron.

In the ninth, after Northrup's homer, Smith sent Mickey Stanley up as a pinch hitter. The first pitch was visibly wide, but deemed a strike by Salerno. Smith yelled something from the perch in the third-base dugout.

Salerno then called the next two pitches strikes, both not swung at by Stanley. Both appeared wide of the outside corner. Salerno's calls seemed to be punitive action by an umpire.

Stanley argued and Salerno gestured him back to the dugout.

Smith was enraged after the game.

"Excuse me, gentlemen," he said to the writers, "I might say something I don't want to."

He left his carpeted office and took a shower. Later he huddled for an hour with Campbell and Rick Ferrell, the old catcher who was a club vice-president. Then he went upstairs with a few friends.

Eventually, during the conversation, there was a Tiger version of the transcript of Salerno's discussion with Stanley at home plate.

"Blame your manager," Salerno was alleged to·have told Stanley after calling him out on three pitches that were outside the strike zone.

The Tigers decided not to file a complaint. It would only make things worse the next time.

Besides, the Tigers had retained the one-game lead they had over the Twins before the series started. But the Orioles now were a perilous half-game behind the Tigers.

MAY 3

The Tigers were knocked out of first place tonight. The Angels did it to them, the same club that did it last year.

Baltimore won and was leading the league.

The Tigers started hitting some. Al Kaline had three hits, Willie Horton had three with two home runs. The Tigers scored five runs, the first time in seven games they could score more than two. But the Angels scored six and Mickey Lolich was the loser and the Tigers no longer were leading the league.

MAY 5

The losing streak was three games, four losses in the last five. Mayo Smith was threatening lineup changes.

Yesterday when Jim McGlothlin beat the Tigers, 7–2, they didn't even bother to remove their bats from their shoulders.

"Six called out on strikes?" said Mayo. "That's nothing new. That's an everyday occurrence."

And so it was Denny McLain's assignment this Sunday to stop the Tigers from another tailspin. He did, beating the Angels, 5–2.

McLain was a four-game winner now—four straight complete games, solo performances with no relief needed. Suddenly he again was the best right-hander in the American League.

So it was natural for the writers to crowd around him in his corner of the clubhouse. Denny spoke and the wires carried his soliloquy:

"Detroit has the biggest front-running fans in the world.

"Cash and I were going bad last year and they got on us real bad. How do they think a guy's wife feels after he goes zero for eight or zero for sixteen and the fans boo while she's in the stands?

"If they think we're stupid for playing this game, how stupid are they for watching us?"

Somebody stopped writing in his notebook to ask if the fans' actions had affected the Tigers in the 1967 pennant race.

McLain continued, "I think it did. There were certain guys on this club who didn't want to go out and play last year because of the fan abuse.

"Now the fans are on Kaline. He's produced for fifteen years, and he'll produce again this year. They don't realize how good a ballplayer he is.

"I don't care if I get booed here the rest of my life. Detroit is a great town. I like it. I bought a home here and have roots.

"But the fans in this town are the worst in the league."

One writer also quoted McLain thusly: "I'd hate to have to win it for these fans."

A few minutes later most of the writing audience had left. McLain spotted Tom Loomis of the Toledo *Blade* still in the clubhouse.

"When I said that," McLain told Loomis, "I meant only one percent of the Detroit fans."

But the damage was done: Denny wasn't quick enough. His comments already were headed around the country via the wire services. He was contrite, but it was too late.

But really, much of what McLain said had truth to it.

Al Kaline was being booed because he was batting .241 with only two runs batted in through 22 games. For some obscure reason, Kaline never quite received the adulation in Detroit that he merited.

The city—the fans, that is, and more than one percent of them—creates heroes. Then when the heroes do not perform quite up to expectations they are booed.

It has happened in baseball long before Kaline. Hank Greenberg was booed and so was Ty Cobb. Bobby Layne would be booed while all the time leading the Lions to world football championships.

Booing is inherent in Detroit, and now Denny McLain had left himself vulnerable to it.

But meanwhile McLain had arrested the slide with the Tigers trailing the Orioles by a game and a half. This was important because the Tigers were starting a three-game series tomorrow in Baltimore.

MAY 8

In the major leagues each hitter is different. Just as no two sets of fingerprints can be perfectly matched, neither can two hitters. They vary in style, and some hit well only when a hit would be unimportant. Others hit in streaks and then slump and then hit in another streak. Some have the unexplained knack of hitting whenever a hit is vitally needed.

This is the clutch hitter, and it is into this category that Jim Northrup fits the best. He is a clutch hitter and also a streak hitter.

At the beginning of the season Northrup failed to hit safely in his first twelve at-bats. That really is not too unusual. But in Northrup's slump, he struck out six times and grounded into three double plays in the dozen at-bats.

Northrup cracked the slump with a poorly hit bloop single over the second baseman's head in the fourth game. Since then he had done more hitting than any of the other Tigers.

His batting style is distinctive. He bats left-handed in a manner baseball men term an inside-outside hitter. His hands and the knob seem to be far ahead of the thick part of the bat. He has a corkscrew stance, and when he unwinds he often will hit the ball to left field rather than pulling to right.

In Baltimore, Northrup again saved the Tigers from the ignominy of being no-hit victims.

The first night of a three-game series Dave Leonhard defeated the Tigers with a one-hitter, 4–0. It was the second time they had been so restricted in 25 games. Both times the prospective no-hitter, the first by Hargan in Cleveland and the second by Leonhard, had been broken up by Northrup.

Poor Joe Sparma was pitching some of the finest baseball of his life. But he was the opposing pitcher against both

Hargan and Leonhard in Baltimore. His support for his last four appearances was a sum of two runs. And one of these had been driven home by Sparma's own pinch hitter.

The Tigers were sinking, suddenly two and a half games behind the Orioles. It was the furthest they had been behind. The situation was not especially hopeful. The Tigers had lost four out of their last five.

The next night the game went into the ninth inning without a run scored. Lolich was pitching against Tom Phoebus, who had pitched a no-hitter ten days before against Boston.

The Tigers had endured 17 innings without a run when Willie Horton led off the ninth with a walk.

Mayo Smith commanded Norm Cash to bunt. This was sound strategy, but had perhaps a 50–50 chance for success. Cash possibly could hit a long ball. He also possibly could miss the bunt, because bunting was not one of his specialties.

It worked, and the Tigers had a runner on second. Don Wert was walked intentionally and both runners moved up on Gates Brown's ground ball.

There were two outs, and it was Lolich's turn to hit and he had a shutout. This was the Tigers' best scoring opportunity in two games.

Smith gambled on young Tommy Matchick as a pinch hitter for Lolich. It meant—success or failure—that the bullpen would be responsible in the bottom of the ninth.

Matchick was a gamble because he had hit safely only once in nine at-bats this season. He was not a long-ball hitter, and Smith asked only a single, any kind of single. Matchick lined a double off the base of the right-field wall, and the Tigers had two runs in the ninth.

In the bottom of the ninth Boog Powell hit a homer for the Orioles, but Fred Lasher and Jon Warden kept the counterattack to one run.

The imperiled Tigers escaped, 2–1, with Last Licks Victory Number Eight.

Again Wally Moses, the coach, was credited.

"He told me I was swinging too hard if I hit the ball to the fence," said freckled, rust-haired Tommy Matchick, the Tigers' Huck Finn. "Wally likes me to hit line drives.

"I went about fourteen for a hundred and four at the start of last year in Toledo, and I was about to quit the game. Then the Tigers sent Wally down to work with me, and he straightened me out. He got me hitting line drives and trying not to hit the fences."

This particular line drive off the fence had kept the Tigers from dropping three and a half games behind the Orioles. Instead, they were a game and a half behind, and maybe turned the other way.

It appeared that way, anyway. Northrup hits left-handers as well as he does right-handers, which is rare for a left-handed batter. In the third game, tonight, he homered off Dave McNally, the Orioles' left-hander, in the first inning.

In six of the first eight innings the Orioles' lead-off batter singled. But Earl Wilson had them shut out. In the eighth they filled the bases with two outs.

Brooks Robinson hit a line drive screeching into center field. Out in the darkness, near the fence, Jim Northrup dove and tumbled and caught the ball.

"When he hit it," Northrup said, "and when I started running, I didn't figure I had a chance to catch it. Then I dove and hit the ground with my shoulder and the ball stayed in my glove. With the kind of webbings they have today, it stayed there."

The Tigers won it, 3–1, because of the home run and catch and fled town only a half-game out.

If they could only get some runs . . .

MAY 10

Al Kaline had been unable to blank from his mind his impending historic 306th home run. He thought about it and he thought about not being able to hit it and he brooded.

For the last 18 games, ever since his last homer, Kaline had not batted in a run. He had only two RBI's and one home run through his first 25 games. He was disheartened. He was not hitting and the Tigers were not hitting.

Tonight Kaline went to the plate in the first inning at Washington with an opportunity to drive in some runs. He did, doubling home two runs. His output for the season jumped from two to four. In the second, he singled home another run. In his third at-bat, he hit a three-run homer.

Kaline had finally hit number 306, tying Hank Greenberg for the most homers by a Detroit Tiger.

Tonight he drove in six runs and the Tigers won, 12–1. The Tigers had fourteen hits. Kaline had three, Northrup three and Freehan three.

Denny McLain breezed to his fifth victory and he was 5–0. And Baltimore was beaten.

The Tigers were back in first place—"To stay," said Bill Freehan.

MAY 12

Mayo Smith's pennant concept is to win every series. The Tigers won two out of three, and the hitting continued.

Joe Sparma was given some support yesterday and he beat

the Senators, 12–2. Fifteen precious hits, with Freehan again getting three.

Today the Tigers lost, 6–3, but they were going home in first place with a two-game lead.

And the bats were booming. In the first two games at Washington they scored 24 runs. In contrast in the 12 games before that, they had scored 28.

The Tigers, a month into the season, were assembled the way Mayo Smith planned it.

MAY 14

"We're more maneuverable this year," said Mayo the Magical Maneuverer.

Tonight the Tigers played their twenty-ninth game. Smith employed his fifteenth different lineup. What he wanted most was an everyday first baseman.

"Can you play first base?" he asked Detroit's strike-idled baseball writers. Then he walked out of his office and asked the question of Bill Freehan. Actually it was more of a command.

So Freehan joined the committee that was playing first base for the first-place Tigers. He became their fifth first baseman of the year against the Orioles tonight. Mickey Stanley, Norm Cash, Eddie Mathews and Tom Matchick had been tested there previously.

Only heavily booed Norm Cash was a first baseman by profession.

Freehan turned to Stanley and said, "Let me use your first baseman's mitt, Mick." Stanley eagerly tossed it to Freehan. Matchick, just as eagerly, returned the first baseman's mitt he had borrowed earlier from Mathews. The Tigers were becoming a well-knit team, sharing things and the like.

Smith wanted another right-handed batter in the lineup against the Orioles' Dave McNally. He wanted Jimmie Price to play. But Price cannot play first base. It would be a way to rest Freehan a little bit, too, reasoned Smith.

Neither Price nor Freehan got a hit. But Willie Horton hit two home runs off McNally and Earl Wilson shut out the Orioles, 4–0.

Two years ago the Orioles had won the World Series with McNally their pitching star. That season Horton tagged him for five home runs.

"That was two years ago," said Willie Horton. "You never can look back."

Willie Horton had come out of a Detroit ghetto to play major league baseball. As local prep star he had hit a tremendous home run for Northwestern High School in the city championship game at Tiger Stadium.

Horton had spent the winter recovering from his foot surgery and touring the city's schools.

"Work hard, take care of yourselves," advised Willie Horton.

Tonight one of his two home runs off McNally went 430 feet into the upper left-field seats. As he returned to his position, Horton was given a standing ovation by the fans in the left-field stands.

Most of those cheering were white. The healing process in Detroit had begun.

MAY 15

While the Tigers were on the road, Mayo Smith called Denny McLain in and gave him hell for his impromptu remarks about Detroit's fans. At least for the versions that were printed. The Tigers' front office was deluged with telephone complaints from the baseball customers. The club felt its image had been harmed.

Smith, the maneuverer, arranged for Denny to appear on broadcaster Ernie Harwell's pregame show. There Denny repeated his amended version that only a small segment were bad fans. He again claimed he was misquoted.

Tonight McLain made his first appearance before the Detroit fans since he had maligned them. One hundred percent took it personally. His reception was a mighty chorus of boos.

In the first inning Boog Powell, an old tormentor, smashed a three-run homer off Denny. The fans were more generous with their boos. In the second inning the Orioles scored again. Mercifully, Smith pinch-hit for McLain after the second inning when he trailed, 4–2.

Baltimore won the game, 4–2, and McLain incurred his first defeat after five successive victories. He was now 5–1, an excellent start, and except for tonight had pitched the best baseball of his life.

MAY 17

Joe Sparma once played quarterback for Ohio State. He had a strong arm and liked to pass. But his coach at Ohio State, Woody Hayes, was the inventor of the three-yards-and-a-cloud-of-dust theory. Hayes hated passing. Joe Sparma never really liked Hayes.

So he signed with the Tigers before he finished college.

Mayo Smith, in times of deep meditation, would wish he could have seen Joe Sparma play football. Smith quite frankly wondered how Sparma could have been a football player. The manager never considered the pitcher that much of an athlete.

Tonight, for the second time this early season, Joe Sparma carried a no-hitter into the seventh inning, against Washington. The first time he did, he lost the game to the Yankees. Ken McMullen broke up tonight's attempt for a no-hitter with a home run in the seventh.

In the ninth, Frank Howard swung lazily and tapped a home run liner barely over the left-field screen. Suddenly Washington was ahead and Sparma behind, 3–2.

"I never want to go for a no-hitter again," Sparma swore as he walked through the tunnel connecting the dugout to the clubhouse. "I don't want any more of those ——— things. I always lose them."

The radio was on when he got there, and the Tigers were batting in the bottom of the ninth. Sparma paid little attention to Ernie Harwell's broadcast. He was too occupied throwing his glove and kicking a stool around the room.

Norm Cash singled in the Tigers' ninth and was sacrificed ahead. The Senators brought in a tiny rookie left-hander, Steve Jones, just promoted from Buffalo. Jones induced pinch hitter Mickey Stanley to roll the ball right back to him. Sparma tipped over a stool. But Stanley's grounder kept rolling, right through Jones' legs, and Mickey was safe at first. Jim Price followed with a pinch-single to tie the game at 3-all.

The Tigers then proceeded to load the bases, and now Sparma was very attentive. Jim Northrup was coming up.

"All I need to win it is a fly ball," Northrup reminded himself.

He swung and missed. Then he swung and connected. Northrup hit a vicious liner, pulled off the left-hander, into the upper right-field seats.

The grand slam gave the Tigers Last Licks Victory Number Nine, 7–3.

When Northrup danced through the clubhouse door, Sparma, the old quarterback, handed him a carton of cooled beer.

"I fainted on the floor when he hit it," said winner Sparma.

Joe Sparma liked to blow bubbles, and he would also blow off steam as the season progressed.

"I brought him a six-pack, really I did. I'd been sore as hell and I think he deserved it."

Across the room, holding a can of beer, Northrup disclosed, "I was just trying to hit a fly ball."

"Yeah, sure he was," said Al Kaline, a couple of stalls away at the double locker in the corner. "Did you see that first swing, how hard he swung?"

MAY 19

Frank Howard, a gentle slugger of Bunyanesque proportions, was in Detroit terrorizing the Tigers' pitchers.

Asked if they had talked about Ohio State, which both attended, Joe Sparma said, "I don't want to say anything to Howard. He might kill me."

Yesterday he clubbed two home runs off Mickey Lolich. One cleared the left-field grandstand, a double-decked structure 82 feet high and 340 feet from home plate. There had been just one prior home run over the left-field grandstand at Tiger Stadium by Harmon Killebrew six years before.

Before today's doubleheader, Howard had hit 10 homers in his previous 6 games, driving in 17 runs. Doing so, he broke one of Babe Ruth's minor home run records.

"I have no aspirations of becoming somebody I'm not," said the giant. "This is my ninth season in the major leagues, so I don't kid myself. I have no reason to think I'll be a record setter now. I never have before."

"This year he might hit seventy homers," said Sparma.

But today the Tigers cooled him off, keeping Howard without a home run for the first time in a week.

Mayo Smith dominated a long discussion with Les Cain, the

rookie left-hander, before starting him in the second game. Howard, naturally, figured to be the subject.

"Are you kidding?" said Mayo. "I didn't even mention Howard. It might have psyched the kid."

So young Les Cain went out and recorded his first major league victory, 7–0. He needed help from Fred Lasher over the last two and a third innings, but the kid won. In this game, Al Kaline hit a pinch-hit homer. It was his 307th, and in his sixteenth season he had succeeded Hank Greenberg as the Tigers' number one home run hitter.

In the same game, Eddie Mathews, relatively new to the American League, hit his 510th home run. He now was one behind Mel Ott for sixth place behind Babe Ruth on the all-time home run slugger list.

The first game was another of those typical victories for the Tigers. Washington tied the game with four runs in the eighth. Gates Brown won it, 5–4, in the bottom of the eighth with a single. It was just as simple as that and was Last Licks Victory Number Ten.

The Tigers could leave for their long road trip comfortably in first place after winning the doubleheader. Cleveland now was second, two games behind. The rest were four games back or farther.

MAY 20

Of the other clubs, the Tigers feared and respected the Twins the most.

"They're the best club on paper," said Bill Freehan. "But what's paper?"

The Twins, who had shared second with Detroit a game behind Boston last year, endeavored to bolster their relief pitching during the winter. They traded for reliever Ron Perranoski but had to give up Zoilo Versalles, their disgruntled shortstop. Consequently, their inner defense was now suspect.

Tonight the Twins' infield permitted the Tigers to score two unearned runs. Denny McLain was pitching for the first time since he was bombed out last week by Baltimore. He permitted Rich Reese to hit a three-run homer, and the Twins had nothing more entering the ninth inning. But they led, 3–2, when the Tigers came to bat.

Willie Horton immediately sent the game into extra innings with another late home run.

In the tenth, Al Kaline reached second when Jackie Hernandez, the Twins' new shortstop, fired an errant throw toward first. Bill Freehan, the next batter, grounded the ball to third base, where Ron Clark fumbled it. Kaline scored the winning run.

It was Last Licks Victory Number Eleven for the Tigers, who also had twelve more conventional victories. McLain, again a beneficiary, was 6–1.

The Tigers now had won nine games by one run, each of the nine in their final turn at bat. They were sharing the hero's burden. Freehan, Horton and Brown had each delivered the deciding blows in two of these one-run victories. Northrup, Wert and Matchick were the decision makers in the other three.

MAY 25

Even before their first visit to the new Oakland ball park, the Tigers had been informed about the vision problem for the batters. They complained about the reflection of the sun.

It was especially poor for twilight games. While they concluded the series in Minnesota with two last licks losses, the Twins told the Tigers about the new park. Catfish Hunter had pitched a perfect game against them there, and they complained of difficulty following the pitched ball.

The Tigers' first game in Oakland last night and a California rain terminated the game in the seventh inning. The score was tied, 2–2, and the game would be made up in September.

But the Tigers lost Earl Wilson. He jammed his foot on first base. Tonight he showed up at the park for the twilight game vaulting himself along on crutches.

As the low sunlight streaked across the Golden Gate and glared off the white center-field backdrop, the pitchers dominated the evening game. Lew Krausse was pitching for the A's. On one of his pitches, Al Kaline leaned and was struck by a ball he could not see. It hit him on the right forearm, and he had to leave the game.

The injury caused some ruffled feelings among the Tigers. There had been a lingering feud between the Tigers and A's. Last year they had brawled when the A's were in Kansas City.

Neither Denny McLain nor Krausse had been nicked for a run going into the eighth. Then McLain bunted for a single and scored on a single by Mickey Stanley, who had replaced Kaline.

McLain had to work out of a jam in the ninth, striking out Reggie Jackson, to win his seventh game, 2–1. He was the first in the American League to win seven.

In fact, McLain was the Tigers' only winning pitcher over the last five games. He won with the support of six hits once and five the next time. It looked like another period of trouble for the Tigers with Wilson on crutches and Kaline's arm paining him and other hitters not hitting again.

MAY 26

Early this Sunday morning Al Kaline flew home to Detroit escorted by general manager Jim Campbell. Kaline's right arm had a hairline fracture and he would be lost to the Tigers for three weeks, possibly longer.

Mayo Smith held sick call before the ball game with the A's.

Kaline was gone, Wilson was hurt, and Dick McAuliffe reported in with a bruised thigh.

McAuliffe, quick to heat his temper, had been injured in a freak way. He had struck out and thrown his bat to the ground. The bat retaliated by bouncing and striking him across the leg. He could not play.

Willie Horton was added to the list early in the game. He aggravated his foot while running out a bunt, a surprise tactic for a plodding runner. He made it safely to first and to second on a wild throw. But he had to leave the game.

Soon the A's had a 6–0 lead. The Tigers scored two in the fifth and had four in the sixth to tie the game when Jim Northrup came up.

Jack Aker was pitching for the A's, and he was angry because the game had been tied.

He pitched and the ball cracked Northrup in the back of the head. Northrup crumpled, dazed, then quickly arose. He charged the mound and started pummeling Aker. The dugouts emptied and a 15-minute free-for-all was under way.

The best punch was thrown by Eddie Mathews, who had rushed from the Tigers' dugout. He caught Aker below the right eye.

Aker fell beneath a pile of scratching, clawing, kicking ballplayers. Nearby, Northrup also was down, falling from the momentum of his own rush—and Mayo Smith's attempted tackle. Aker was scratched and battered. The right side of his flashy A's baseball suit was torn into shreds. His leg was gashed in five places.

"This was the best fight I have ever seen on a baseball field," said Ed Runge, who was the home plate umpire. "I mean, there were more punches thrown and landed."

At the height of the battle, Willie Horton was seated in the whirlpool bath at the Tigers' clubhouse, treating his foot. He jumped out of the metal container, put on his street clothes and ran out onto the field barefoot.

"I had to help that man," said Horton.

Horton, who had been an amateur boxer as a teen-ager, arrived too late. The fight was over.

At the side of the Tigers' dugout some fans started throwing debris at the athletes. Somebody poured a beer into the dugout.

One of the ballplayers, irrationally, picked up a loose baseball and climbed up the steps. He threw it into the grandstand.

Mrs. Mary S. Alamieda, fifty-two, of San Leandro, California, claimed she was hit in the face by the baseball thrown by the unidentified athlete. She would file a $200,000 damage suit, stating the projectile hit her above the eye and cut her.

Northrup was ejected from the game. Runge said he started the fight, and Northrup certainly did not deny that. Lew Krausse, whose pitch had broken Kaline's arm last night, also was ejected for improper language. The A's John (Blue Moon) Odom also was ejected.

Odom and McAuliffe had been combatants last year in a similar beanball epic. So today they sought each other again. Odom was ejected, the umpires said, for kicking McAuliffe in the ribs.

After the game, won by the A's, 7–6, in the tenth inning, Aker telephoned Northrup.

"I reminded him that he was digging in at the plate and I had to knock him down," said Aker. "I told him I had no intention of beaning him, that the pitch sank on me. I was trying to brush him back, but the pitch didn't sail. It sank and Northrup ducked right into it."

Northrup returned from a hospital X ray examination with a headache and bruised knuckles.

"He deliberately threw at me and hit me in the head," said Northrup, his temper aroused again. "A hitter's got to protect himself. When I was down I felt like I was going out. Then I got up and thought that they'd been throwing at Willie and Al.

"We've had a lot of people thrown at all year. When they throw at your head, you've got to do something about it. If they hit me in the head, I'm going to go out there again. I got in a couple of good punches before Mayo and the umpires got me down.

"It's okay if they try and brush you back, at the legs. But throwing at your head can cost your entire career.

"I've got to keep playing, because Al's out now."

Back in Detroit, Jim Campbell put Kaline in the hospital, and he was placed on the disabled list. Wayne Comer was brought up from Toledo to replace Kaline numerically on the roster.

"They were disturbed Saturday night when Kaline was hit," said Campbell. "I say let them go. They're a spirited ball club."

The Tigers' outfield for three weeks or more would be Horton in left, Stanley in center and Northrup in right.

They would have to continue the pennant race without Kaline, their best all-around player. They were struggling already, with three losses in the last four decisions—and all three in the other teams' last licks.

Today Mayo had to scrounge. Bill Freehan, the catcher, finished the game as the right fielder. Mickey Lolich and Dennis Ribant, a relief pitcher, were employed as pinch hitters. Denny McLain was a pinch runner.

The Tigers headed south to Anaheim with their lead in jeopardy.

MAY 30

At Anaheim it got closer. The first game of the series again went into extra innings. And again the Tigers lost, 7–6, to the Angels in the twelfth. This was their fourth loss in five games. The worst part was that Mayo Smith had made another correct prediction. The Tigers now were losing games as they had been winning them just a few days before. All four of these losses were in the last innings. It hurt deeply because guys like Rene Lachemann of the A's and Tom Satriano of the Angels—second-liners—were the men who stabbed the Tigers in these late innings. They make dubious heroes.

In their mixed-up way, the Tigers had a genuine hero in defeat. Eddie Mathews socked two home runs. They were numbers 511 and 512 of his career, and he went ahead of Mel Ott as sixth man on the all-time home run listings.

But the Tigers had only a half game left of their lead over Baltimore.

"One thing about this club," said Mayo Smith, "is it has been through troubles before. What they went through last year is helping them this year."

Some of the Tigers spent the next day visiting Disneyland, which was not far from their hotel in Anaheim. It was much too early in the season for brooding.

That night the slumping Tigers returned to the ball field known as the Big A to face the Angels once again. Opposing them was George Brunet, a longtime nemesis. They had Brunet out of the ball game in one-third of an inning. Bill Freehan drove in two runs with a double, and Willie Horton, playing on his gimpy foot, followed with a two-run homer. John Hiller, the Canadian left-hander who was little used by Mayo Smith, pitched from the second inning on to win the game, 4–1.

But Baltimore won, too, and the Tigers still had only their half-game lead.

Denny McLain protected the Tigers. Last night he shut the Angels out with five hits. It was his best game of the year as he advanced his record to 8–1, and it was still May. He struck out three Angels in the 3–0 victory, and Horton hit another two-run homer.

Horton, in a hot streak, stands close to the plate and is knocked down often. The time after his homer he went down again. Horton dusted himself off and turned to the catcher, Satriano.

"If the next one's close, I'm going to punch you in the nose," said Willie to the catcher.

The next one wasn't close.

Baltimore lost and the lead was stretched to one and a half.

The Tigers flew home tonight, turned about again, with a new winning streak, now three games. Freehan and Northrup hit home runs and Joe Sparma won, 7–3. It was a cheerful flight across the country, and back home the Tigers had a four-game weekend series coming up with the Yankees.

It should be the first big attendance series of the year. The people of Detroit, accustomed to the Tigers collapsing in late May, were getting grandiose ideas about their ball club.

Maybe they could win the pennant. Maybe.

MAY 31

Willie Horton was born in Arno, Virginia, a mining hamlet. He was the last of nineteen children. When he was eight, the Hortons moved to Detroit. Willie grew up in what today is called a ghetto. It was—and still is—an area where poor black people lived. He had a normal childhood for a boy growing up in that environment as part of a very large family.

At an early age Willie learned how to hit—with a bat and with his fists. He was encouraged to use the bat, and when he was fourteen, Louis D'Annunzio, a scout for the Tigers, first saw him on the sandlots. D'Annunzio wrote the name of Willie Horton down in his future book.

Willie went to Northwestern High, at the corner of Grand River and West Grand Boulevard. He played ball on Northwestern Field, next to the old high school. Many major leaguers had been graduated from Northwestern Field, with its several rocky, lumpy diamonds.

While at Northwestern, Willie aspired to be a boxer. When he was fourteen he entered a Golden Gloves tournament in Windsor, across the Detroit River in Canada.

"I'm eighteen," said Willie, and he was permitted to fight.

At home, Clint Horton flicked on the television set and tuned in the channel showing the fights.

"That's Willie fighting, isn't it?" said Mr. Horton.

The Hortons did not care for their son to be a boxer. That night when Willie returned home, his boxing career was quickly ended by his mother. He was told to concentrate on baseball.

At sixteen, Horton, playing for Northwestern High in the city championship game, lined a home run into the upper right-field deck at Tiger Stadium.

He played on a national championship sandlot team when he was seventeen, in 1960. A teammate was Bill Freehan. The team was to go to Pennsylvania by bus for the national tournament. Departure time was nine in the morning from Northwestern Field. When the other players arrived to go aboard the bus, they found Willie asleep on a park bench at the field. He'd been there since five thirty.

"Didn't want to miss the bus," said Willie.

In August of 1961, Willie Horton signed with the Tigers for what was reported to be $50,000. He was eighteen. That December, Willie got married.

He was twenty and had played for Duluth, Syracuse and

Willie Horton

Malcolm W. Emmons

Knoxville when the Tigers called him up for the first time. It was September of 1963.

On September 14, Clint Horton, Willie's father, paid one dollar for admission to the bleachers at Tiger Stadium. Willie had asked him if he wouldn't prefer a free ticket in the grand-stand behind the Tigers' dugout at third base. Mr. Horton told his son he'd rather sit in the bleachers, that he'd always watched the Tigers play from there.

It was a tight ball game with Baltimore. The Orioles led, 2–0, in the eighth. Robin Roberts, the great right-hander, was pitching. It was late in Roberts' career, but he still was a good pitcher, able to get the hitters out.

Charlie Dressen, the Tigers' manager then, already was rav-ing about Horton, although the youth had been with the club only a few days on the road. Dressen was like that—enthusias-tic about the prospects of kids he felt he could help become major leaguers, such as Horton and Denny McLain.

With Roberts beating the Tigers by the two runs, Dressen told Horton to grab a bat and pinch-hit for Jim Bunning. Horton walked to home plate for his first at-bat in his home-town as a major leaguer. A Tiger was on base.

One hand was holding the bat as he swung at Robin Roberts' pitch. The ball was driven—lined—into the upper left-field seats. As Willie Horton jogged around the bases with his first major league home run, Clint Horton jumped in the bleachers, clapping his hands. Others around him also jumped. The game was tied, 2-all.

"That's my boy, that's my boy Willie," yelled Clint Horton —and nobody around him in the bleachers in deep center field would believe what the man was saying.

Horton's home run enabled the Tigers to continue into the tenth inning and they won the game then.

Clint Horton rushed through the corridors of the old ball park and into the clubhouse to embrace his son.

On New Year's Day, 1965, Clint Horton and his wife were driving through a snowstorm on a highway near Albion,

Michigan. There was an accident, and Willie Horton's parents were killed.

Willie Horton joined the Tigers as a regular in 1965. By 1967, when the Tigers barely missed their pennant, they often played without Horton. He missed forty games. A bone spur was causing severe pain in his left heel.

Surgery removed the spur during the winter. This year his left baseball shoe was fitted with a cushion of foam rubber. The rubber lipped over the leather.

But it still hurt a lot. And last Sunday, bunting at Oakland before the fight, he hurt it again. The next night he was back in the lineup anyway. Eight pills a day diminished the pain.

"His injuries are something we'll have to live with, I guess," said Mayo Smith.

Tonight there were 31,000 customers in Tiger Stadium to welcome the Tigers on their return from the West Coast. Mel Stottlemyre was pitching for the Yankees against Mickey Lolich.

It was 0–0 in the seventh inning. Stottlemyre now had to face Horton. The duel went to a 3–2 count, with the last three pitches smoking fastballs. Now Stottlemyre shook off his catcher's signal for another fastball. He wound up and threw a curve.

Willie drilled it over the left-field fence, and the Tigers won their fourth straight, 1–0.

The spectators stood and cheered and yelled as Willie limped around the bases on his aching foot with the game's only run.

"The noise is nice," said Horton. "It inspires me."

"You've got to give him credit," said Stottlemyre. "He hit my pitch."

Willie Horton, whose sore heel had held him to 19 homers all last year, finished up May with 14 for the new season. He hit a dozen this month, three in the past four games. His hitting streak was 13 games.

JUNE 1

"This is awful, this is awful," said Mayo Smith, grimacing his face into that anguished, hawklike look.

"Wert has a bad back and Mathews is hurt too. We can play around Kaline, but not Wilson. We have enough out-fielders. But Willie's heel hurts, too. These things catch up with you."

With Wilson's foot still bad, Smith started Les Cain against the Yankees. The Yanks quickly got five hits off the young-ster and three runs, and he could retire only one of the six batters. Pat Dobson, a tall, right-handed relief pitcher, was rushed in. Smith had called on Dobson for only 12 innings of work during April and May, fewer than anybody on the staff except Dennis Ribant.

Mayo needed a pitcher in an emergency, and he was gam-bling. The first batter Dobson faced, Bobby Cox, got the sixth hit of the first inning and drove in the fourth run.

Dobson never did allow another hit. A pitcher with a de-liberate windup and an overhand motion, he kept the Yankees from adding to their run tally through the second, third, fourth, fifth and sixth innings. It was the most he had worked all season.

The Yankees led, 4–2, when the Tigers batted in the bot-tom of the sixth. Willie Horton led off with his fifteenth homer, his fourth in five games. Norm Cash followed with his third homer to tie the score, 4–4.

In the seventh, Jim Northrup singled and stole second. The Tigers didn't run much; this was only their ninth stolen base of the year. It became the winning run, 5–4, when Bill Free-han singled in his third run of the game. Freehan, in turn, was thrown out at the plate, tearing his baseball pants, on Horton's third hit of the game.

But it didn't matter. The Yankees got only one more hit after the first, a single in the ninth off Fred Lasher.

The Tigers' winning streak was at five, and they were opening up the pennant race. Their lead was three and a half games, with Baltimore, Cleveland and Minnesota, all losers today, tied behind them.

The statisticians started keeping track of a new dimension. This was the fifteenth game, of the 29 won by the Tigers, which had been won in the seventh inning or thereafter.

"Maybe we're not good front-runners," said Freehan, who'd won this game. His uniform was filthy and torn at the left knee. "It's good to be dirty when you win."

Across the clubhouse, picking soiled stockings and stuff off the carpet, John Hand's lined face broke into a grin. Hand had been the Tigers' clubhouse man for many years. He had a philosophy about things, but he didn't say much.

"These guys can't lose," Hand said to a sportswriter. "They're just like Boston last year."

"They'll still find a way to lose," replied the cynic. "They always do."

"They won't find one this year," said Hand.

JUNE 2

Mayo Smith is not a rhubarb manager. He doesn't go out and harangue the umpire in the manner of Leo Durocher. He does not attempt to expose the umpire as does Eddie Stanky. He does not kick his legs and attempt to drop-kick his base-ball cap as does Ralph Houk.

But umpires are managers' natural enemies, and Mayo Smith occasionally does dispute their decisions. He'll go out and crane his neck toward them and spew some words, presumably many of them harsh. If he is really sore, he'll swing his arms downward in angry gestures to emphasize the correctness of his argument.

Quite often, though, Mayo Smith will saunter out and question the umpire, receive an explanation and saunter back to the dugout.

It was to Mayo Smith's credit that as the manager of the Phillies, the Reds and the Tigers, he never had to be ejected from a game.

Until today.

By the eighth inning of the first game of the doubleheader with the Yankees, Denny McLain had squandered a 3–1 lead with his home run generosity. It was tied, 3–3. Then Tom Tresh broke the tie in the ninth with a run that the Tigers believed never scored. He was on third and headed home on Bobby Cox's grounder to shortstop.

Jim Price, catching, was a yard in front of the plate when Tresh slid into him. Price had the ball, thrown to him perfectly by Ray Oyler. Tresh slid, right into Price's glove. He was obviously out.

Bill Kinnamon, the plate umpire, spread out his palms and yelled safe.

A few moments later Smith had been ejected for the first time in his career.

So the Tigers lost, and their five-game winning streak ended. McLain did not lose, but he did not win. He left for a pinch hitter in the eighth, and Jon Warden incurred the last licks loss. Warden, the relief hero of April, discovered the major leagues were not Utopia after all. His record was now 3–1.

Smith continued to fume between games. Earlier in the day, before the first game, he had ribbed Houk, the Yankees' manager, about his difficulties with the umpires.

"You probably won't last the day," said Smith the needler.

Smith faked a dropkick of a baseball cap.

Now he and Houk took their lineups to the umpires before the start of the second game. Houk, with some difficulty, maintained a poker face. Mayo also said nothing, looking at Houk's expressionless face and knowing exactly what he was thinking. As the meeting broke up, Mayo leaned over and whispered: "And the hell with you, Houk, you ———."

Smith started John Hiller for the first time this season. The Tigers were in the midst of a burdensome stretch of the schedule. It was worsened by Earl Wilson's unavailability. Hiller could throw hard, but Smith seldom was inclined to pitch him. Today Smith had no other choice.

Hiller went the distance and beat the Yankees, 8–1, with Mickey Stanley hitting a grandslam home run.

That had a calming effect on Smith—until he saw a photographic strip which pictorally supported his argument with Kinnamon.

JUNE 6

Five games in four days in Boston had Mayo Smith scrambling for pitchers. The Tigers were in the midst of a 17-day period without an off-day, and without Earl Wilson.

While the Tigers were in Boston, Senator Robert Kennedy was assassinated in Los Angeles. This had a saddening effect on a team struggling.

Joe Sparma lost the first game in Boston, 4–3. The last licks magic did not work. The game ended with the Tigers failing to score the tying run from third base against Sparky Lyle in relief.

The next night the Tigers lost the first game of a twi-nighter to the Red Sox, 2–0. Mickey Lolich pitched a two-hitter but lost it. Again the Tigers failed in the ninth. Lyle again got the last Tiger out leaving two base runners.

From their five-game winning streak, the Tigers suddenly had dropped three of four.

Smith again had to raid his bullpen for a starting pitcher in the second game. It was Dobson, who had started only one major league game before—last year. Don Wert helped him with a home run, and Dobson won, 2–0.

Still strapped, Smith asked Denny McLain to pitch the next day with only two days' rest. McLain agreed and was rocked for three runs in the first. His arm was tired, and in the seventh he trailed, 4–1. It was his last inning because Smith planned a pinch hitter.

McLain went back to the clubhouse, presumably beaten for the second time.

In the Tigers' seventh, Wert led off with a grounder to third, which Joe Foy booted. Tommy Matchick, playing shortstop, singled. Dick Williams, the Red Sox manager, lifted starter Ray Culp and brought in Bill Landis.

Landis got three balls on Dick McAuliffe and then threw a fourth one that was a wild pitch. Another run scored. Williams again changed pitchers. He brought in Jim Lonborg, last year's pitching hero who was just returning after his skiing accident.

Lonborg did exactly what Williams wanted him to do. Mickey Stanley hit a grounder to shortstop. But Rico Petrocelli threw the ball away and two more runs scored for the Tigers.

In the clubhouse, because of two errors and a wild pitch, McLain became a 5–4 winner instead of a loser. Helped by faultless relief from Daryl Patterson over the last three innings, McLain now was 9–1 for the season.

Today Smith had to go back to Sparma, who lost the series opener. Sparma also was operating on two days' rest, one fewer than was customary and two fewer than was preferred. He gave up two runs in the first as the Red Sox matched Jim Northrup's two-run homer. Sparma then gave up another in the second. But in the third, Norm Cash propelled a three-run homer to put the Tigers in front, 5–3. It remained that way as Sparma, tired, staggered into the ninth. Fred Lasher rescued him and got Elston Howard for the final out with the bases loaded.

The Tigers headed back to Detroit with three straight victories—somehow.

JUNE 7

They were coming out to watch the Tigers, and tonight another crowd of more than 31,000 welcomed the team back from Boston. They came with grocery sacks filled to the handles and with brown bags under their arms. Their mood was as if they were going to attend an orgy.

The Cleveland Indians were the opposition, so it was the first-place team against the second. The Tigers' lead was two and a half games entering the three-game series.

Before the game, the people straddled their bundles on the concrete ledges and stood for a moment of silent respect to Robert F. Kennedy.

Then the game began. By the fifth inning, with Don Wert and Tom Matchick misplaying the ball, the Indians had a 3–0 lead off John Hiller. Steve Hargan, the Indians' right-hander who had one-hit the Tigers in April, had a no-hitter into the sixth. Dick McAuliffe ended the suspense with a line single in the sixth. But in the bottom of the seventh the Indians still led, 3–0, and Hargan had a one-hitter.

Then Norm Cash, badly booed and benched so often, hit his fifth homer. Up stepped Willie Horton, hitless in 16 at-bats, 1 for 23 since his 14-game hitting streak was snapped. Horton whacked his sixteenth home run to left. It was suddenly 3–2, and Alvin Dark, the Indians' quick-change manager, switched pitchers.

A managerial duel—Mayo Smith vs. Dark—suddenly developed as an underplot.

Hal Kurtz, Dark's second pitcher, hit Tom Matchick to put two Tigers on base, still in the seventh. With one out, Smith ordered Jim Price to bunt the runners ahead. But Kurtz got two strikes on Price, nullifying the bunt situation. Smith promptly employed Rule No. 1 of the manager's guidebook. With the 0–2 count, he sent Gates Brown up to face Kurtz. He wanted a left-handed batter hitting against the right-handed pitcher.

Dark immediately counteracted, as specified in the guidebook, Rule No. 2. He took Kurtz out and brought in a left-handed pitcher, Mike Paul, to pitch to Brown. Smith declined the next move and the game was allowed to proceed.

Paul completed the strikeout against Brown. With Price out of the game, Bill Freehan would have to catch despite a bum hand. So Smith sent him up as a pinch hitter and Paul struck him out on a called third strike.

The Indians still led, 3–2.

In the bottom of the eighth, Paul retired the first two batters. Then Cash came up. He tied the score with his second homer of the game. The crowd cheered as Cash trotted around the base paths, and he merely looked at the ex-booers seated near the dugout.

Up stepped Willie Horton. Dark trotted to the mound.

"Walk him," commanded Dark. Paul looked quizzically at his manager. There was nobody on base. Horton would become the possible go-ahead run.

"Walk him," said Dark.

Paul deliberately threw four pitches out of the strike zone and Horton walked. He then struck out Don Wert.

It was three apiece starting the ninth inning. Paul led off by working Fred Lasher for a walk. Two of the cardinal sins of baseball are walking the opposing pitcher and walking the first batter of an inning. Lasher had double-sinned.

Dark had Larry Brown bunt to advance Paul to second. Paul stayed there when José Cardenal scratched a single off Lasher's glove.

Malcolm W. Emmons

Norm Cash

But then Tony Horton singled to right. Paul ran around third and dashed for home. Jim Northrup, in right, fielded the ball and threw toward the plate. Freehan took the throw at the edge of the plate. Paul slid. Freehan put the tag on Paul's baseball shoe.

Jim Honochick, the umpire at home plate, jerked his thumb up. Paul was out. Then Honochick spread out his hands, palms down. No, Paul was safe. The tie had been broken.

Bill Freehan is the ideal size for a tight end, which he played one year at Michigan. He wheeled and pushed Honochick, driving the umpire backward. Mayo Smith ran from the dugout, aware he had no catcher to replace Freehan. Smith wrestled Freehan away. The manager is not the size of a tight end, but nonetheless Smith shouldered Honochick back with a strong block. Freehan was prevented from making further physical contact, but he continued to sass Honochick. Smith tried to quiet Freehan and argue with Honochick at the same time. He waved his arms. Freehan kept yelling.

Honochick kept saying Freehan juggled the ball, that Paul was safe, that the run counted. Bill Valentine, the third base umpire, attempted to pull Smith away. It was a tug-of-war. Valentine yanked Smith's arm. Smith yanked back.

"Get your ——— hands off me," hollered Smith.

"I'm keeping you out of trouble," said Valentine.

"I'm already in trouble," said Smith.

But the run counted, and Mayo Smith—for the second time in his career, for the second time in five days—was ejected from a ball game. Freehan, for some reason, was not.

The crowd erupted. Beer bottles, crushed beer cans, fruit, eyeglasses and liquor bottles went flying. The people booed and screamed, and objects from the second deck landed perilously close to the athletes on the field. Spectators started punching one another in the grandstands.

Out in the right-field bullpen, Bill Rohr, a relief pitcher, started to warm up for the Indians. He was unable to because of the debris thrown at him.

"Has the whole world gone crazy?" said Rohr. "In the stands there were a couple of guys standing together, slugging ... really hitting each other. There was a group of people beating up on an old man.

"This is nuts."

The Indians had the lead and loaded the bases, and there was still only one out in the ninth. Dark ordered Max Alvis to bunt and he did. Back to Lasher. Lasher threw to Freehan for a force-out at home plate. Freehan relayed to Dick McAuliffe covering first for a double play on Alvis.

But the Indians had that one precious run, a 4–3 lead.

The crowd continued to throw their garbage onto the field. Honochick called the press box and asked for an announcement. Joe Gentile, the PA man, asked the people to stop, to show Detroit sportsmanship. The crowd booed and threw more things.

From right field, Tommy Harper of the Indians came into the dugout to get a protective batting helmet, then returned to his position. A beer can, crushed and sharp-pointed, hit Joe Azcue, the catcher, in the arm. The thrower was off target. He had aimed at Honochick. Somebody scaled a cigarette lighter from the upper deck.

"I was scared out there," said Larry Brown, the Indians' shortstop. "Nobody could stop them."

Bill Valentine, the umpire, picked up a pair of spectacles. Somebody had thrown them at him. Somebody else threw a quart beer bottle at him. It was full.

Amid this scene of near-riot, Mike Paul went to the mound to protect the Indians' one-run lead. He struck out Matchick and got Dick Tracewski on a grounder to Brown at short. Two outs, none on.

Freehan came up, and Alvin Dark, the computer spinning beneath his red baseball cap, walked to the pitcher's mound. Back to the guidebook. Freehan batted right, Paul pitched left.

Dark called for Stan Williams, a right-hander, to face Freehan. But he might still need Paul. So Dark took his first baseman, Tony Horton, out of the game. He sent Paul to play first base while Williams pitched to Freehan.

Williams got two strikes on Freehan. One more and the Indians would win. Freehan tapped the next pitch into left field for a single.

Dark came out again. He sent Paul back to pitch and stationed Lee Maye, an outfielder, at first base.

Again the guidebook was all-powerful. Paul, left-hander, vs. Dick McAuliffe, a left-handed batter. Still the Indians needed just one more out, and still the stuff came from the stands.

Smith, the ejected, crept down the dimly lighted corridor between the clubhouse and the Tigers' dugout. A cigarette was cupped in his hand. He was not supposed to be this close to the dugout, but . . .

Paul pitched and McAuliffe rolled a ball to the right of first base. Maye, the outfielder, stepped over and bent to pick up the ball and get the third out. As he leaned, Maye booted the baseball, his foot kicking it toward second base. McAuliffe was safe at first on the error and Freehan reached second.

Mickey Stanley came up, and the Indians still led, 4–3, with one more out needed. Smith edged closer through the darkness, almost to the end of the corridor and the steps up to the dugout.

Paul got two strikes over, and Smith was closer to the dugout. Stanley hit the next pitch, foul, toward left field. José Vidal came over to try to make the catch. But the ball curved into the grandstand. Smith now was at a vantage point where he could see the batter. Stanley fouled another pitch off.

Then he swung again but did not hit the ball very well.

The ball floated lazily over the second baseman toward right center field. Cardenal, the center fielder, was pulled to left. He was running and Freehan and McAuliffe were running.

The baseball dumped into short right center and bounced.

Smith was in the dugout. Freehan scored easily with the tying run. McAuliffe was churning on the 270-foot route from first.

Mac, make them make a play on you, Mayo Smith thought the instant Stanley hit the ball. *Make them throw you out at the plate.*

Cardenal reached the ball. He fumbled it. Finally he threw. The ball traveled weakly and inaccurately. It didn't matter. Dick McAuliffe crossed home plate with the winning run, 5–4.

At the pitcher's mound Mike Paul stood silently. He was stunned. He finally walked to the dugout.

The crowd erupted with cheering. Jim Honochick, as soon as McAuliffe touched home plate, walked toward the Tigers' dugout and to that same corridor which also leads to the umpires' room.

The Tigers were on the field, and Freehan had Stanley on his shoulders.

Honochick did not see Smith. As McAuliffe touched the plate, Smith turned and retreated down the corridor and sank into the soft swivel chair in his office. It was several minutes before his players trooped into the clubhouse.

Freehan slumped in front of his locker.

"Comeback wins like that are beautiful," he said, his round face glistening. "The most beautiful thing in the world. Even umpires can't beat us when they make lousy calls.

"I shoved Honochick. I shoved him halfway across the world. He said I was juggling the ball. The runner really was wiggling his foot. How could I juggle a ball in my bare hand?"

The question went unanswered.

"I guess he would have been within his rights to throw me out," Freehan said. "But you think, we lost the pennant by one game last year, and who can say which was the one game that cost us the pennant?"

Mayo Smith's face was red. There was still anger.

"I'm not happy," he said. "This is the second time in a week I've been kicked out. Everything is the umpire's judgment. He said he juggled it. There's no way you can juggle a ball in your bare hand. Here, try it."

Mayo picked up a baseball and put it in his right hand and demonstrated.

"If I do juggle it, it's out of my hand."

The ball dropped to the carpet.

"I had to get out there fast, or Freehan and Cash are out of the game," said Smith.

Somebody asked Smith where he was when Stanley hit his triple and McAuliffe scored the winning run.

"I'd rather not say where I was," he said, breaking into that gargoyle grin.

"Did you see it?"

"Oh, yeah, I saw it," said Smith.

"Did you get into that celebration?"

"No, I didn't come out for the celebration."

In the other clubhouse, behind the first base stands, Alvin Dark sat on a stool in front of his locker. His fine hands occasionally rubbed through his curly black hair. He sat doing this, head cast down, for a long time, perhaps half an hour.

Dark spoke, finally: "The violence of the people in the stands didn't beat us. We beat ourselves. All of us."

All of us—a manager, too, who puts an outfielder at first base in a very pressurized situation.

"The ball kept carrying away from me," said little José Cardenal, the Indians' fastest runner. "If I catch it, we win. If I don't, we lose."

"I thought it was going to be caught," said Mickey Stanley, who had hit the ball. "First, I didn't know whether to take the pitch or swing."

Norm Cash was practically overlooked. He had hit two home runs—three in two days to contribute to two victories. He had the people cheering. It was different.

In 1961, Cash had won the American League batting championship with a .361 average. Every year thereafter he had struggled, never rising above .279. Last year Cash had been benched in the pennant stretch. He had been booed terribly and angered when he did not play. He batted .242, and during the winter the Tigers tried to trade him and get a new first baseman.

They were unsuccessful, and Smith decided, according to the guidebook, he could play Cash against only right-handed pitchers. Cash was mixed up and even had problems hitting them.

Now, for the first time since 1961, Cash was on a solid hitting spree.

"I knew I was better than what I was doing," said Cash, the Texan. "I couldn't get myself together. I made a few adjustments. I'm moving my bat back farther. I'd been jumping my bat at it too much."

Another endorsement for Wally Moses' batting instruction was anticipated.

"I did it myself," said Norm Cash.

It was mentioned to Smith that Cash finally had started to hit. Smith nodded.

"I might add, it's time," said Smith. "If we can get some hitting at that first base spot, it will help."

Tonight's game was Last Licks Victory Number Twelve.

JUNE 8

Robert F. Kennedy's funeral was today. Baseball decided to play no baseball until the assassinated Presidential candidate was buried at Arlington. The Tigers changed their day game to a night game.

The funeral was far behind schedule. The train bearing Senator Kennedy's body from New York to Washington was slow and late.

At eight o'clock more than 28,000 fans were in the grandstand at Tiger Stadium. The players talked solemnly in the clubhouses.

The Tigers talked mostly of last night.

"My wife saw my mouth moving," said Bill Freehan of his engagement with Jim Honochick, "and said I was using words she didn't even know I had in my vocabulary."

Norm Cash was exercising his vocabulary. He had been benched against a left-hander, Sam McDowell. Freehan was at first base.

The ball game started while the funeral continued.

Mickey Lolich beat McDowell, 3–1, and the Tigers had a five-game winning streak and a four-and-a-half-game lead over Cleveland.

JUNE 9

President Johnson had decreed this Sunday as the national day of mourning for Senator Kennedy.

Baseball had decided to play its schedule. A few major league ballplayers balked. Nobody on the Tigers or Indians refused to play.

The Tigers had decreed today as Bat Day. A crowd of 52,938 was at Tiger Stadium.

Luis Tiant was the only pitcher in the American League close in the victory pursuit of Denny McLain. Today they opposed each other—and on the field it was not Bat Day.

McLain gave the Indians three hits through eight innings. Duke Sims doubled in the fifth and scored on Joe Azcue's single. In the seventh, Sims got the third hit, a home run. McLain left for a pinch hitter, trailing 2–0 in the eighth.

Tiant permitted the Tigers only four hits and pitched his fifth shutout. It was his ninth victory, matching McLain. Denny now had lost for the second time.

JUNE 12

The business-sport of baseball is full of clichés:
Wait till next year.
The game isn't over until the last man is out.
I can't get to first base with him.
A baseball takes funny bounces.

They are a part of the American language. The funny bounces were particularly apt with the Minnesota Twins, in town for a four-game series. This was the team the Tigers felt would challenge them most seriously for the pennant. But their respect for the Twins was already waning.

Last night there was a twi-night doubleheader which lasted until early this morning, and there were funny things that happened.

Pat Dobson, who had been in some disrepute until he emerged when Earl Wilson was hurt, had a stretch of 23 scoreless innings. It ended when Tony Oliva hit a home run in the eighth inning of the twilight game. By then Dobson had a 3–0 lead.

An error by third baseman Rich Rollins and some boomer-anging strategy presented him with two gift runs. The Tigers had runners on second and third following the error, and there were two out. Cal Ermer, the Twins' harried manager, decided to pitch to Jim Price with first base open. Most managers would have walked Price and pitched to the opposing pitcher, Dobson.

Price singled to left, scoring the two base runners.

Dobson, with relief from Daryl Patterson, won for the second time during the pitching shortage, 3–1.

Cesar Tovar's error on a ground ball permitted the Tigers to score a run in the third inning of the second game.

But the Twins had a 2–1 lead going into the eighth.

Young boys who discuss baseball during schoolyard recess periods always come up with riddles. Such as: How can a team send six batters to the plate in an inning, have five of them reach base and score only one run?

In the eighth inning Mickey Stanley led off with a single which Ted Uhlaender permitted to roll through him in center for an error. Ron Perranoski, the relief pitcher, balked Stanley to third. Jim Northrup struck out, but Perranoski's third strike was a wild pitch. Northrup ran to first and was safe. Two on, none out. Norm Cash singled in Stanley with the tying run.

Al Worthington replaced Perranoski and struck out Willie Horton for the first out. In doing so, he threw another wild pitch and Northrup and Cash advanced. Freehan then walked to load the bases.

Mayo Smith had Don Wert attempt to bunt—and Northrup was out at the plate on the suicide squeeze. Two outs. Wert then hit the ball between short and third and Cash dance-stepped trying to get out of the way. But it hit him for the third out. Because it hit a base runner, Wert was credited with a single, his first base hit in 20 at-bats.

And that was how the Tigers answered the riddle of getting five of six men on base in an inning and scoring only one run.

It was after midnight when the Tigers batted in the ninth. Tommy Matchick and Dick McAuliffe both singled. But Worthington did precisely what he wanted to against Mickey Stanley. He forced Stanley to bounce a double-play ball to Jackie Hernandez at short.

Hernandez flipped to Tovar at second. Tovar's relay

skipped past Harmon Killebrew at first, and Matchick came in with the winning run.

The 3–2 victory was Last Licks Number Thirteen for the Tigers. The Tigers scored six runs in winning the two games. Four of the six were unearned.

Tonight two runs were sufficient. Mickey Lolich dueled Jim Kaat, 1–1, into the eighth. Kaat did not permit the Tigers a hit between the second and the eighth.

Then McAuliffe, hitting left-handed, cracked a home run, and the Tigers won, 2–1.

It was Last Licks Victory Number Fourteen. It was the twentieth victory earned after the Tigers had been either tied or behind as late as the seventh inning. That was more than half their 38 victories. Of these, 16 were by one run.

The Tigers had won 14 of their last 18 games, and the lead over Baltimore grew to five games.

"I don't think people give these guys credit enough after what they went through last year," said Mayo Smith. "They grew up a lot."

There was still another casualty. Eddie Mathews, the vital left-handed hitting veteran, would be lost—maybe for good. Mathews was placed on the disabled list. He needed surgery for a herniated disc in his back.

JUNE 13

Tom Loomis had a pertinent comment about the new math for Denny McLain.

McLain had just beaten the Twins, 3–1. Two of the Tigers' runs again were unearned, because of Jackie Hernandez's error at shortstop.

"Denny, you've won ten games in one-third of the season —that works out to thirty victories," said Loomis.

It was mathematically sound reasoning. Nobody had won 30 games in 34 years, since Dizzy Dean. But McLain did have an impressive start. He was 10–2.

Loomis, known as Ace to his colleagues, is an imaginative, redheaded baseball writer from Toledo. He made the drive 60 miles up the freeway to cover the Tigers. He waited to record McLain's reaction to his mathematical projection.

McLain's eyebrows jumped up. He was silent for perhaps a half second.

"It works out to eleven," said McLain. "I've got a helluva shot at eleven. I tried that two years ago. I had thirteen in a half year. It worked out to twenty-six. I thought. I just got in the back door to twenty."

"The red hair, what happened, Denny?"

McLain was no longer a redhead. The long, straight red hair had been cut. Denny again had a blond-brown, close-cropped Princeton cut.

He again said the sun in Florida had turned it red, not some concoction from a bottle.

"I did not dye my hair, no matter what anybody says," said McLain. "It was Mother Nature. I had it cut Tuesday."

"Why?"

"Because it's hot out there."

There remained some fan reaction to McLain's published remarks about their loyalty.

McLain disclosed that someone had put a smoke bomb under the hood of his family automobile. It was discovered when Sharyn McLain drove into a gas station with daughter Kristin, two.

The attendant discovered it when he opened the hood to inspect the oil gauge. The smoke bomb had been wired incorrectly.

"If the bomb had gone off when my wife was driving at a high speed on the highway, she and the baby could have been killed," said McLain.

"If anything had happened, I'd have spent the rest of my life finding out who did it."

The Tigers had swept the four-game series from the Twins although they couldn't score more than three runs in any game.

"When you get eleven runs and win four ball games, that's a tribute to your pitching," said Mayo Smith. "Fortunately for us, Hernandez has played pretty good for us . . . and Tovar, too."

The Twins scored only five runs in the four games. They could now be considered out of the pennant race. The Tigers had shoved them eleven games out. Baltimore was five and a half behind in second.

"Mayo," said a writer, "you're killing the pennant race."

He contorted his face in that agonized expression saved for when he is being put on.

"Oh, come on, Jerry, come on," he said, affixing his tie and heading for another confrontation with Eddie Stanky.

The Tigers flew off to Chicago with 15 victories in their last 19 games.

JUNE 14

Mayo Smith had discovered another statistic of success.

"We've won twelve of the thirteen games when Price was catching," said the maneuverer.

When Price caught, Freehan transferred to first base, and a left-hander opposed the Tigers. Freehan had been a first baseman, mostly, the last several days.

It was getting to be time to think about the All-Star game next month in the Astrodome. So Freehan was stirred into response by the statement: "You can either be the All-Star catcher or the All-Star first baseman. Which would you rather be in the All-Star game?"

"I don't want to make it," he said. "I'd rather have the three days off."

Last year Freehan caught all 15 innings of the All-Star game without relief. He did not care for such prolonged duty and said so. He played tired throughout the second half of the season.

"Well, isn't there value being on the All-Star team?"

"No," said Freehan. "You go up there at the end of the year to talk contract and they tell you you had a good first half, that's all. In the All-Star game, you catch fifteen innings and don't get anything for it, except maybe a gift."

Tonight Freehan started at first base for the third straight game. Price caught.

The pitcher was Earl Wilson, back after an absence of three weeks.

Eddie Stanky's club was out of last place, finally, and up to ninth.

The White Sox jumped on Wilson, with three runs in the first and another in the second. Gary Peters held the Tigers hitless into the fifth. Then Freehan singled and so did Willie Horton. Peters walked Price, filling the bases. Ray Oyler drove a sacrifice fly deep to left. Then Wilson hit a 3–2 pitch through the strong wind off Lake Michigan for a three-run homer to tie the score.

It went into the thirteenth, 4–4. Mickey Stanley was on first and Jim Northrup came up. Northrup was in one of his valleys. He had gone hitless for 21 straight at-bats. Northrup singled Stanley to third. Freehan then broke the tie that had lasted six innings with a single, his third hit.

Pete Ward, an old friend, had a hand in it. Freehan's single, hit hard, went off Ward's glove at third.

But there was retribution. In the bottom of the thirteenth, Ward tied the game, 5–5, by slashing the ball off Norm Cash's glove.

In the top of the fourteenth, Don Wert hit the first pitch for a home run. The Tigers had their third winning streak of five games in three weeks. They had won 10 of 11, 16 of 20, and they were 6–0 over Stanky's White Sox. They were in first place by six and a half games, and it was just mid-June.

Stanky had used 20 of his 25 players attempting to salvage the 4-hour-and-12-minute game. He was silent again.

It was Last Licks Victory Number Fifteen.

JUNE 15

"Stanky orders his pitchers to hit someone whenever he thinks the time is right," Tony Cuccinello had said.

Cooch had said this at the start of the season, when there was an outbreak of headhunting in the league. He said it after Carl Yastrzemski had been hit by a pitch, the first pitch after Stanky had gone to the mound to talk to his pitcher.

Cuccinello had been third base coach under Stanky before Mayo Smith hired him in Detroit in 1967.

Joe Sparma was the pitcher today for the Tigers. Stanky started Tommy John, a left-hander who wore mod clothing and was the White Sox's most effective pitcher.

In the second inning Bill Freehan hit a home run. Willie Horton, the next batter, was hit in the shoulder by a pitch. Three batters later, John hit Don Wert, last night's hero, in the leg with a pitch.

Sparma had difficulty with his control. Two walks in the fifth filled the bases, and Ken Berry cracked a grand slam homer.

In the sixth, John hit Horton again with a pitch and then Ray Oyler, who had to leave the game. Four Tigers had now been hit by pitched balls, and Stanky removed John from the game with a 5–1 lead.

Freehan had three singles after his home run. McAuliffe and Horton also homered. But the White Sox broke the spell and defeated the Tigers, 7–5. John was 5–0 for the year.

The five-game winning streak was over.

On this afternoon, Mickey Stanley made the finest catch Mayo Smith ever saw. Stanley ran 60 yards diagonally across right center and made a diving catch of Tom McCraw's drive. He tumbled onto the gravel track, arose and doubled Luis Aparicio at first base. He was limping but waved off Mayo and trainer Bill Behm.

"Stanley's a helluva key for our ball club," said Smith.

"You've been winning without Kaline, what do you do when he comes back, he's almost ready?" said a sportswriter.

"I'll worry about that when he's back," said Smith. "I sure wish he was back now. I know what I'd do if he was ready now."

"What?" said the agitator.

"Kiss my butt," said Mayo, contorting his hawk face. "His arm's not ready yet."

"You don't have to throw much at first base," said the writer, reading Smith's feelings about the situation there and the difficulty of breaking up the new outfield combination.

"Stanley's catch," countered Smith. "He went down into the gravel and cut his knee. He said, 'I'm okay.' I could see his pants torn. He should have had stitches. But the meat was all torn, the stitches wouldn't hold. It was bad. What a catch."

JUNE 16

The Tigers and White Sox split their Sunday doubleheader today. Eddie Stanky had a parting message for the Tigers, who opened their lead to seven and a half games over the Orioles.

"I said last year they should have won by ten games," said Stanky. "Now I say the Tigers will win it big . . . or they'll lose it big. Why do I think so? I'll tell you why when they win it or lose it. They know why.

"They're running scared and it's only June. Guys like Horton, Freehan and Cash bunting for base hits. If that isn't an indication of what I mean, I can't tell you any more.

"The Tigers will be the disgrace of the American League."

Mayo Smith maneuvered again today. With Ray Oyler knocked out of the lineup, Smith switched Dick McAuliffe to shortstop. Mac became the Tigers' fourth shortstop of the season. Tom Matchick played second.

The Tigers lost the first game, 3–2. Mickey Lolich, once called a second-line pitcher by Stanky, was the loser.

Denny McLain pitched the second game and held the White Sox to one run and three hits for seven innings. But the Tigers scored none. Again McLain would have to be lifted for a pinch batter.

The first three Tigers reached base in the eighth, and it was none out when Smith sent Horton up to bat for McLain. Stanky counterattacked by lifting Cisco Carlos and bringing Hoyt Wilhelm in to relieve.

Willie hit Wilhelm's knuckle ball through the middle, just meeting the ball as he was taught. The ball rolled 60 feet to Wilhelm, who fell down. Horton had an RBI single and the score was tied. Wilhelm went to 3–1 on McAuliffe, and Stanky made another change. He brought in Wilbur Wood, a left-handed knuckle ball artist. Wood finished the walk to Mac, forcing in another run, and the Tigers led.

Northrup, still slumping, doubled in two more runs. Cash then singled in the fifth run of the inning.

The Tigers won, 6–1, and McLain again got the victory after he had been taken out for a batter. He was 11–2, and he had some explanations for his record.

"I'm keeping the ball down," he said. "For the first time

in three years, I have no arm trouble. This is no alibi. But I can throw hard on every pitch.

"More than that, I've gone back to my side-arm fastball. It's another pitch. I have more command of my pitches, better concentration.

"I was a little bit mixed up last year. I was bothered by some things outside of baseball. It bothered my concentration.

"Charlie Dressen taught me most of what I know about pitching now. He taught me off-speed pitching. I had no curve ball when I came up and he taught me that. He was like a father to me.

"Now I think we're going to be okay with Mayo. We used to try to go .500 on the road, and if we did we thought we were playing pretty good ball. Last year we tried to get two out of three, three out of four. Now we go into a city and say we're going to go four out of four."

Mayo Smith had nothing to say about what Eddie Stanky had to say. Denny had something to say.

"Stanky got the most out of his pitching staff last year," said McLain. "He got too much out of them last year. He hurt them. They don't throw as hard anymore."

Denny sort of got in the final word.

JUNE 18

The Tigers were whipping the league by eight games entering the three-game series with the Red Sox. Just how they were eight games in front defied the analysts.

You looked for reasons in the statistics and that only deepened the mystery. Only one Tiger was batting better than .300. He was Gates Brown, the irregular who had contributed as a peerless pinch hitter.

Otherwise, Willie Horton had the highest average at .289 and Bill Freehan was batting .285. Al Kaline was next at .257, and he hadn't played for three weeks and was still on the disabled list.

Mickey Stanley was hitting .243 and Dick McAuliffe .241 and Jim Northrup, with his hots and colds, .235. Don Wert was .225 and Norm Cash was struggling, despite his recent surge, at .197.

Mayo Smith was rotating men at shortstop—and Tom Matchick had a .213 average, Ray Oyler .148, and Dick Tracewski .170.

The starting pitching was equally mysterious. Denny McLain was 11–2, but the other three were struggling merely to have winning records. Mickey Lolich, who traveled to the ball park on his motorcycle, was 5–4, Earl Wilson 4–4 with another start tonight, and Joe Sparma, quickly falling into disfavor, 5–6.

So it wasn't the hitting and it wasn't the starting pitching either.

"It's been the bullpen," said Mayo Smith, who had created the bullpen himself. "It's given us the ability to stay close. It had to perform the way our starters have done—only .500 except for McLain."

It figured—a strong emergency pitching job kept the scores close. Close enough for all those histrionics in the late innings when the batters suddenly would defy their own averages.

John Hiller and Pat Dobson had been asked to perform double duty, starting and relief. Their pitching was vital in the spurt to the eight-game lead.

Hiller, from Scarborough near Toronto, cost the Tigers nothing, just the ink in the pen he signed with. He didn't receive a bonus. Dobson, from upstate New York, had signed for a bonus of $25,000.

"I spent it all on cars and fast living," Dobson would say, "and I enjoyed every second of it."

Fred Lasher cost the Tigers $4,000 in purchase money from the Twins' organization.

"Dobson's game in Boston, when he beat them after they'd beaten two of our starters, was the most important game so far," said Wally Moses, the coach. "Dobson is winning the pennant for us."

He was only 2–0 and he didn't have a save yet. But statistics could not disclose how important he had been. Hiller was 5–1 and Lasher 4–1.

Tonight's game with the Red Sox, the pennant defenders, emphasized the contribution of the bullpen.

Wilson pitched magnificently against the Red Sox. He usually did against his former team. The Tigers rewarded him with a 2–0 lead.

Northrup doubled home one run in the first. The cause was abetted by the special cop in the left-field corner who sat on a stool and was assigned to pursue adventurous fans and stray foul balls. Northrup's fair ball veered toward him and he danced to escape. At the same time, he delayed Carl Yastrzemski's effort to retrieve the ball. Stanley thus was able to score from first on the double.

Willie Horton sent in the other run with a looping single after an error and some lethargic base coverage.

It could have just as well been runless in the ninth.

Yaz was the first batter and Wilson walked him, throwing the first two pitches into the dirt. The first pitch to Ken Harrelson was wild, and Yaz advanced to second. Smith jumped up from his special platform seat at the front of the dugout and walked stiff-legged to the mound. He jabbed out his arm and beckoned Dobson.

Wilson, angered last year when he was yanked prematurely, simmered and left the mound.

Harrelson then singled to center and Yaz scored. Reggie Smith also singled. The Red Sox suddenly had a run home and runners on first and third.

Late last September the Tigers had lost two games in this

very manner to the Red Sox. They would have won the pennant if they had won just one of those two.

Smith stuck with Dobson. Rico Petrocelli, the next batter, slapped the ball back to Dobson. Harrelson ran and was trapped between third and home and run down. One out.

Dalton Jones batted for Mike Andrews, the left-handed percentage again against the right-handed pitcher. But Jones was special to the Tigers. He thrived against them, he murdered them. Dobson struck Jones out with his overhand fastball. Two out.

Dobson then struck out Jerry Adair for the final out and saved the victory for Wilson.

Smith vaulted off his platform and leaped up the steps. He thrust his clenched right hand skyward.

"I wanted to win that one," said Smith. "Boston came in here rather cocky. They'd just won three straight, and this took something out of them."

There was another reason for the eight-game lead. Baltimore and Cleveland had simultaneous losing streaks while the Tigers were winning. The Orioles lost five straight, the Indians seven. Both broke their losing streaks tonight. So the Tigers remained secure, eight games ahead.

JUNE 19

Still there were certain tensions, just an uneasiness that could be felt some nights at the Detroit ball park.

"We're coming out to your neighborhood and burn down your house. We'll get your wife and kids."

One of the Tigers, who had this yelled at him, disclosed it to Joe Falls, sports editor of the *Free Press*.

"He has to be scared," Falls said gravely.

Joe Sparma was Mayo Smith's starter tonight—and the Red Sox loaded the bases with none out and Ken Harrelson singled in a run. Then with the bases still filled, Sparma struck out the side.

That erratic inning became the pattern for the night.

By the seventh inning, the Tigers had a 4–2 lead. Sparma had two outs and a runner on base. Joe Foy bounced the ball back to Sparma. He went one way, the ball another, and Foy had a scratch single. Harrelson followed with a three-run homer to put the Red Sox ahead.

Smith's face turned crimson when it happened. In the eighth the Red Sox scored three more runs. Daryl Patterson walked the first two batters and then threw a bunt away with a high throw when he had a play at third base.

It was sloppy play. The Detroit fans were not unforgiving even with their team eight games in front.

Beer cans and fruit came out of the grandstands. Then in right field a firecracker exploded. Then another blast.

Ken Harrelson, the Hawk, a man with long sideburns and a vast wardrobe, stood in right field. He was petrified.

Suddenly he leaped forward. An instant later, where he had just been standing, there was the loud report of a cherry bomb. Then a puff of white explosive smoke.

"That cherry bomb hit me right in the back," said Harrelson. "It fell between my legs and exploded. It scared the hell out of me."

Bill Valentine, the home plate umpire, had Joe Gentile plead with the fans over the public address system.

"Your attention, please. Detroit has a reputation for good sportsmanship . . ."

There were some boos. Displays such as this had been going on at the ball park ever since the people threw Depression-purchased vegetables at the Cardinals' Ducky Medwick in the 1934 World Series.

The game continued, and suddenly another explosion occurred over Harrelson's head. He started the walk in from right field, waving his arms. He threw his glove. He was leaving.

At second base, umpire Al Salerno stopped Harrelson and persuaded him to remain. He did, playing 15 feet behind second baseman Mike Andrews. On the next pitch Don Wert struck out to end the game, an 8–5 victory for Boston.

"No wonder they have trouble in this town," said Harrelson. "It's people like that, just a few jerks, who give a city a bad name.

"If there hadn't been two strikes on the hitter and two outs, I would have walked out. That could ruin your career. One of those things in your ear could kill you. If anybody got one in the face, it'd blind him.

"This is the only town where that stuff happens."

John Wyatt, a veteran relief pitcher acquired so Les Cain could be farmed out, remembered things like this in Boston. Wyatt was with the Red Sox last year when they won the pennant.

One day he was warming up and the bleacherites started throwing coins into the bullpen at Fenway Park. Wyatt gathered up the donations that had been thrown at, not for, him.

"Going to give that to the Jimmy Fund?" inquired a Boston writer, mentioning Boston's and Ted Williams' favorite charity.

"No," said Wyatt. "I'm taking it to the dog track."

Wyatt did and lost the entire bundle, $88.

Jim Campbell, the Tigers' general manager, was concerned about the bombings. Harrelson had not been the only target. When the Tigers were in the field, some of the firecrackers exploded near Jim Northrup.

"These people are drunks all steamed up," said Campbell. "We don't sell beer in the stands. You have to get it at the counters, and it's sold in paper cups. But people bring beer in with them. They make themselves something like a money belt and tie the beer cans around them. We take some away at the gates, but we can't frisk thirty thousand people as they come into the park.

"We have plainclothesmen sitting in the crowd up there, but plainclothesmen won't stop it. A fan can walk along and flip one out of the stands and nobody can say who did it. They can light the fuse with a cigarette and be gone by the time it explodes. The fans sitting nearby could help, but they won't. Nobody wants to get involved. Nobody wants to go down as a witness."

Mickey Lolich, the National Guardsman, also had a thought.

"That kind of stuff has TNT in it," said Lolich. "A guy doesn't need basic training. Just play the outfield in Detroit."

"They're going to have to spend some money and put cops there," said Mayo Smith.

He was unhappier about the ball game, particularly the way Foy's bouncer to the mound eluded Sparma.

"My follow-through took me to my left and I tried to reach back and the ball hit my leg," explained Sparma.

"He doesn't know what he did," growled Smith.

JUNE 20

The Tigers announced there would be extra special police in the stands. Patrons carrying paper sacks and the like to the park would have them scrutinized. Nobody would be permitted to carry in cans or bottles of beer or pop.

On the sidewalk along Trumbull Avenue, outside the main gate, the people milled around, shuffling to get inside. Denny McLain was the drawing card tonight. In an entranceway somebody trying to avoid detection merely dropped a heavy paper bag to the sidewalk.

The glass from a half-gallon jug fragmented on the side-

Mickey Stanley

—Malcolm W. Emmons

walk, and red wine trickled through the cracks in the pavement. A group of fans, all swigging Canadian beer from
bottles, stepped around the glass.

At the entrance hundreds of confiscated bottles and cans
were lined up on the pavement in disorderly ranks.

But inside it was orderly.

Denny McLain pitched no-hit ball until the seventh. He
walked Rico Petrocelli on a disputed pitch with two out,
and then George Scott lined a single to left, the ball grazing
off the tip of Ray Oyler's glove as he leaped.

McLain finished with a three-hitter, winning, 5–1. He was
12–2. Mickey Stanley had a home run, double and single and
drove in four runs.

The lead was eight and a half games as McLain stood sip-
ping his cola and answering the questions.

"What did you say when Scott broke up your no-hitter?"

"I just went like this," McLain said, dropping his shoulders.
"And this," snapping his fingers. "And I said *fudge*."

"You got a lousy call from the umpire on that pitch to
Petrocelli, eh, Denny?"

"I didn't say that," responded McLain. "Mr. Campbell, I
guess, wants me to be a diplomat. I just have a bad habit of
saying what I believe."

"What about your contact lenses?"

"I have a tinted one in this eye [left] and a clear one in
this eye. The only reason is I lost one of the tinted ones."

"Do they help your pitching?"

"I haven't seen in four years."

"What do you see better with them?"

"Things like baseballs. I haven't seen a baseball in four
years."

"When did you start wearing them?"

"Last October, after the season. The day after I got these
things I dropped my glasses and cracked a frame. If I still
had my glasses, I'd probably be wearing them now."

"You got away with putting your hand to your mouth a

couple of times tonight, you know that?" (There was a new rule in effect that a pitcher no longer could touch his hand to his mouth and then wipe it off while standing on the mound.)

"I'm not going to my mouth. I'm scratching my nose. For some reason, when I'm pitching well my nose itches."

"How's your organ playing coming?"

"I'm getting my trio ready for this fall. We're getting bookings ready. We've got a guy on bass, another on drums and me on the organ."

JUNE 21

"Say, Mayo," said Dick Williams, manager of the Red Sox. "You know you don't have it sewed up. I remember a team that had a thirteen-and-a-half-game lead in August and didn't win the pennant. I remember that team because I was on it, the 1951 Brooklyn Dodgers."

The needle penetrated. Mayo Smith thought of Dick Williams' statement as the Tigers left for a five-game series in Cleveland. The Indians, Orioles and Twins were eight and a half games back.

"I'm surprised we're this far ahead," Smith said. "I thought there'd be another dogfight this year when I thought about it last winter. The whole thing now is to avoid a losing streak so the only way anybody could catch us is to jump right out of the pack to get at you."

There was another factor to be considered now with the Tigers so far ahead—the thing Williams meant when he mentioned the 1951 Dodgers. Suppose, just suppose, the lead dwindled to five games, or less. What happens? Panic? A chain reaction? A reversal of momentum?

"If it causes a chain reaction, we're not that good," said Smith. "We're not going to get panicky. Last year helped this club."

"I'd rather be eight and a half ahead than eight and a half behind," said Bill Freehan. "We're in the position where nobody can play just .500 ball to get at us.

"Somebody would have to get superhot, I mean really hot, to get us. We can go out every day and play relaxed.

"If we got supercold, somebody could catch us. So we have to keep going. Without the papers, we don't even know how close they are. Yes, I mean with the papers on strike, it cuts the pressure. If a pitcher's going bad and lost several in a row, he's under less pressure if he doesn't wake up in the morning and have to read about it. If you're in a slump, you don't want to be reminded of it."

So the Tigers breezed into Cleveland's big ball park for five games.

"We can end up anywhere from three and a half games behind to thirteen and a half games," said the Indians' Alvin Dark.

"If we can win two of the five, we'll be okay," said Smith.

In the ninth inning tonight Mickey Lolich had a 2–1 lead. José Cardenal singled, but the Tigers needed just another out for the victory. Tommy Harper's double brought in Cardenal to send the game into extra innings.

The Tigers regained the lead in the thirteenth when Mickey Stanley singled and Jim Northrup doubled. Pat Dobson went to the mound to face the Indians in the bottom of the thirteenth, another last licks victory almost won.

For the second time, the Tigers were one out from winning. They failed to get the out. Tony Horton cracked a two-run homer over the left field fence, and it was a last licks loss instead, 4–3.

The Tigers had lost the kind of game they had won so many times. Their lead was snipped to seven and a half games.

JUNE 23

Baseball had been near death in Cleveland for several years. Once the Indians almost moved to Seattle. But they stayed and the public apathy continued.

But today 44,000 paid their way into the lakefront park. Yesterday the Indians had cut another game off the Tigers' lead with a 2–0 victory. The Tigers had but five hits, as Dark maneuvered four pitchers into the game.

In the first game this afternoon, as the crowd war-chanted, the Indians cut the Tigers' lead to five and a half games. It was scary already with three games cut off the lead so fast. It was another shutout, a three-hitter by Luis Tiant.

Between games, Mayo Smith did some juggling. He put light-hitting Dick Tracewski at second base and took out Dick McAuliffe. He put rookie Wayne Comer in right field and took out Jim Northrup. Smith wanted right-handed batters going against Sam McDowell. He was disenchanted with Joe Sparma but started him and hoped he would last awhile.

It was the chain reaction, so soon after the eight-and-a-half-game lead.

McDowell mastered the Tigers through four innings. They had gone 22 innings without scoring. Then McDowell walked Ray Oyler. Larry Brown, the shortstop, messed up Mickey Stanley's grounder with two out.

Tracewski was no threat. He had a .170 average. In five big league seasons and part of his sixth, he had hit four home runs. Now he faced Sam McDowell, when right a terribly difficult pitcher to hit.

It was a mismatch . . . Tracewski cracked McDowell's pitch to left field and over the fence for a three-run homer. The Tigers had scored.

"Now I have nothing to look forward to the rest of the year," said Tracewski.

Sparma got into the seventh and Smith called upon Pat Dobson, who pitched the rest of the game.

The Tigers won, 4–1, and their lead remained six and a half games, when it could have been four and a half.

"This was our most important game of the year," said Mayo Smith.

Again the Tigers had refused to permit a losing streak to stretch beyond three games. Again they prevented themselves from losing too much momentum.

JUNE 24

Jim Northrup was not hitting well—he'd had but one hit in his last 20 at-bats. He was benched for yesterday's second game because of the slump.

"I don't think I'll play him again tonight," said Mayo Smith, sitting around the Sheraton-Cleveland during the afternoon.

Mike Paul, the lefty, was to start for the Indians, and Mayo again was figuring the percentages.

Before the ball game Smith sat down in the clubhouse and started work on the lineup card. The ninth spot for the pitcher was easy. It was Denny McLain's turn. Smith left right field vacant for a while and then reconsidered. He wrote Northrup's name in there at the seventh spot in the order.

In the first inning Paul walked four men. Bill Freehan popped a single for his first hit after 25 consecutive hitless at-bats.

Northrup came up with the bases loaded. He struck out against Paul.

Jim Northrup

On the dugout steps Mayo Smith cursed his stupidity.

Northrup again came up in the fifth with the bases loaded. Eddie Fisher was pitching. Northrup came out of his slump. He hit a grand slam home run.

In the sixth, Don Wert was beaned and carried from the field. Ray Oyler ran for Wert, loading the bases once again. Northrup again was the batter, and Bill Rohr, a left-hander, came in to pitch to him.

Again Northrup hit a grand slam home run, off Rohr's first pitch. He was only the second man to hit grand slam homers in consecutive at-bats. The Orioles' Jim Gentile was the other, in 1961.

The two grand slams made McLain's thirteenth victory easy. The score was 14–3, and the panic, which the Cleveland paper said was imminent, did not occur. The Tigers had won the two games—the last two—Smith had said would be acceptable.

"I wasn't sure I was going to play," Northrup kept saying again and again. "I came to the park thinking I wouldn't play, and I end up by having my biggest night. I couldn't take much more of this slumping."

It had been another of Mayo Smith's good hunches.

"Yes, I was considering not playing Northrup," said the grinning manager. "I was considering not playing him because he was going horse————."

"Well, what made you change your mind?"

Mayo considered this only a second and said: "I thought the other guy would be more horse————."

The Tigers took off for New York with their lead back at seven and a half games.

JUNE 25

At Yankee Stadium it was monsoon night, and the ball game was held up three times.

By the seventh inning the Tigers trailed, 5–1. The Tigers scored six times, and Willie Horton drove a triple to the center-field monuments 461 feet from home plate.

It was the twenty-second time the Tigers won with a rally in the seventh inning or later. Denny Ribant, in relief, won his first game as a Tiger, 8–5.

JUNE 26

The American League today announced its team for the All-Star game. Willie Horton made it and Bill Freehan was picked as the catcher, not his secondary position at first base.

The rains continued and the Yankees called off the ball game. The Tigers flew home to be the weekend host to Eddie Stanky, their lead eight games over the Twins.

JUNE 29

"Can I get in the record book?" mused Fred Lasher, the underarm relief pitcher. "Is there a category for most games won by a score of five to four? All the five I've won have been by that score."

Lasher won the first game with the White Sox by the 5–4 score last night. After Pete Ward's two-run homer put the White Sox ahead, 4–3, in the seventh, Lasher was called in to replace Earl Wilson. Lasher retired the last nine batters in order.

While he did it, Mickey Stanley hit a two-run homer to give the Tigers one of those seventh-inning-on victories.

It was another angry victory for the Tigers over the White Sox. Joe Horlen, the White Sox's starter, twice hit Willie Horton with pitches. The Tigers did not throw back at the White Sox. Still the beaning of Don Wert in Cleveland was a fresh memory.

"Our pitchers have no orders about retaliation," said Mayo Smith.

But he would prefer they didn't.

"We're getting hit more because we're in first place," Smith said. "We can't throw back because we don't want to stir up the other teams."

There are other ways to get even and make an impression.

Tonight the White Sox gained a 2–1 lead on Denny McLain. In the third, McLain led off with a single and Dick McAuliffe followed with another single. Stanley walked and the bases were filled.

Of course, Jim Northrup hit another grand slam home run off Cisco Carlos into the left-field seats. Never before in the entire history of major league baseball had one batter hit three grand slam homers in the same week.

In the next inning Tom Matchick singled and McLain singled again. The Saturday night crowd of 34,000 stirred as Stanley batted again with two out. They were rooting for a base on balls, nothing else. Jack Fisher complied by walking Stanley—and the bases were loaded once again.

Tumult greeted Northrup as he walked to the plate. Fisher's first pitch was a fastball right over the plate. Northrup let it go for a called strike. The second pitch bounced into the dirt and Northrup took a vicious cut and missed. The third pitch also was in the dirt and Northrup took another heavy cut.

The mighty Northrup had struck out—on three pitches.

McLain coasted onward to his fourteenth victory. The score was 5–2, and the Tigers had another of those five-game winning streaks, the fourth in a month and a day.

"I was trying to hit another one, that's why I struck out," said Jim Northrup in the clubhouse. "You can't hit them when you want to. On the other three, I was just trying to hit a fly ball.

"In Cleveland I realized the situation, but I was just trying to hit the ball hard. Tonight I was with the crowd, I wanted to hit another one. I should have swung at the first pitch.

"Oh, I'll take the one. You don't often get one. It's always a fluke."

Northrup already had four of the flukes this season.

JUNE 30

Last month the Tigers had a two-game lead when Al Kaline's arm was broken. Now it was eight and a half games, and the Tigers had gone 24–12 while he recovered. Soon Kaline would be ready, and Mayo Smith had been mulling the problem of where to station him.

How could he break up the outfield that was winning so many games? What could he do? This is the kind of problem a manager has when his team is far ahead in first place.

Kaline had waited all these sixteen years to play on a pennant winner. Now the team was winning the pennant without his playing.

"I'm not an active part of it," Kaline said, "but I'm still part of it. I think I've helped just by showing up at the games. That shows I care. I could have gone to the beach."

There had been conversation that Smith would play him at first base. Kaline had never played there and preferred to return to right field. But how could Smith take Northrup out of right field now? Kaline said he'd rather start learning first base fresh in spring training.

Today Bill Freehan, the All-Star catcher, started against the White Sox at first base. Jim Price was the catcher. Tommy John was pitching for the White Sox against Joe Sparma.

The statisticians announced the Tigers had played 11–2 with Freehan at first, 17–2 with Price catching.

Sparma brushed John back on his first two pitches to him. It was a small payback for the four batters John had hit two weeks ago. The Tigers did nothing else, and John defeated them, 12–0.

In the second inning Freehan's career at first base suddenly stopped. Price tore a muscle in his leg. Freehan had to go back to catcher.

Eddie Stanky left town gloating.

"I wouldn't let anybody order World Series tickets yet," he said. "I played on a great ball club in 1951, and we were thirteen and some games behind in August. The Giants won the pennant. There's a long way to go."

Smith was concerned about Sparma and was questioned whether he considered transferring the pitcher to the bullpen.

"No," said Mayo at his corner in the pressroom, "because I can't use Joe Sparma in the bullpen. And if you want me to shoot him, you pull the trigger.

"He'll keep starting. If he's right, you might get six or seven good innings. You can't bring him in from the bullpen and think you're all right.

"Besides, he got us over the hump in Cleveland last week.

"But I still want to see Sparma play quarterback. Woody Hayes must be a genius. Joe's passes must have been like this."

Smith's empty hand traveled up high.

"Because he throws like this."

Smith's hand released an imaginary baseball up high.

Smith was asked about Kaline's return. "He isn't going to play for several more days, maybe not until after the All-Star game."

JULY 1

Mayo Smith needed a right-handed hitting first baseman tonight because Bill Freehan was now catching again.

Al Kaline made his debut as a first baseman, the Tigers' sixth first baseman of the year.

Kaline had reported to Tiger Stadium at three thirty to practice.

Al Kaline

"I wanted to do something without anybody watching," he said. "I practiced with some kid, the batting practice catcher."

After practice Kaline returned to the clubhouse to change to a dry uniform. Wally Moses followed him in.

"Don't practice too much, Al," said Moses. "You're playing tonight."

"That was the first I knew of it," Kaline said later. "Mayo had told me he wasn't counting on me until next week after the All-Star game. He said, 'Last year you told me you were ready and you came back too soon.'"

Kaline was a little hesitant in the infield and once was charged with an error when he lifted his foot off the base too soon.

In the sixth inning Mickey Lolich and George Brunet of the Angels were engaged in a 1–1 duel. Mickey Stanley led off the Tigers' sixth with a triple into the right-field corner.

Kaline was nothing for two in his return when he came up as the next batter. Brunet got two strikes on him and Kaline slid his hands up the bat handle, choking up. He swung gently and singled to left, bringing in the tie-breaking run.

Bill Freehan added to the Tigers' lead with his second homer of the game in the eighth. Dick Tracewski also hit one, his second of the year. Lolich went the distance in the 5–1 victory.

"Actually, it was pretty easy," said first baseman Kaline of his new experience. "But I was lucky I didn't have any tough chances and that they didn't have any left-handed batters to hit the ball at me.

"I'm glad I finally could do something. I was afraid when I came back the club would go into a slump and everybody would blame me. A jinx. Last year when I came back I didn't hit at all."

JULY 3

Denny McLain won his fifteenth tonight—with the Tigers three games short of half a schedule. He had lost only twice, and Mayo Smith had said, "I can't expect McLain to keep going the way he has been percentage-wise."

After beating the Angels, 5–2, with a four-hitter, McLain sat by his locker. His face was immersed in a chunk of watermelon and he dropped the pits into a wastebasket between his feet.

Ed Browalski, the huge, good-natured baseball writer for Detroit's *Polish Daily News*, approached.

Browalski: "How was the weather?"

McLain: "It was too cool out there. I stiffen up. I don't like it this cool."

Browalski: "Why you eating the watermelon?"

McLain: "To cool off."

By now a crowd was gathering.

"I don't consider myself the best pitcher in the league," said McLain. "I consider myself the best pitcher in the league on nights when I go out to pitch. I consider Sam McDowell the best pitcher in the league. It's a shame. Some day he'll put it all together, I hope.

"I would like to have a closer pennant race for the people," continued McLain, who has an understanding of showmanship. "I don't want to win it by twenty games . . . like hell, I don't.

"I feel it every time I go out there—keep them close and somebody's going to hit one out of there for you."

McLain had the support of three home runs tonight. Norm Cash hit one. Willie Horton hit one. And the new slugger, Dick Tracewski, hit one. It was the second in two games for Tracewski, third of the year and seventh of his life. A pho-

Dick Tracewski's forte was fielding, but suddenly he had a big two home runs in two games.

tographer took the routine picture of the three home run hitters.

"Tracewski wanted to be in the middle of the picture, holding up the other two," said Mayo Smith.

"If he never hits another one, he's helped us . . . that one he hit off McDowell in Cleveland was the most important one we've had all year. With the Dodgers he played second base and they won the pennant. When Maury Wills got hurt, Tracewski played shortstop and they won the pennant."

Now he was playing third base for the Tigers while Don Wert recovered from being hit in the head by a pitched baseball.

Throughout Detroit, on the side streets and on the expressways, in the suburbs and in the inner city, SOCKIT TO 'EM, TIGERS in bright, luminous colors was appearing on the rear end bumpers of Cadillacs and jalopies.

And tonight a bumper sticker suddenly appeared above the locker of slugger Tracewski.

UDERZ DO NICH TIGERS, it proclaimed. Ed Browalski explained it was a very loose translation into Polish of Sockit to 'em, Tigers.

Denny McLain was still surrounded as he slipped an olive turtleneck over his head.

"You're halfway to thirty, what about it? That puts you way ahead of Dizzy Dean's pace."

"All I'm trying to win is number sixteen," said McLain. "I'm not going to put the kiss of death on myself."

"What about the All-Star game next week? The way Mayo has his rotation you'll pitch Sunday, which means you might not be able to pitch in the All-Star game."

"To me and Mayo the championship season is more important. Number one first is here."

"What about one hundred thousand dollars?"

"The hitters deserve it more, but the pitchers have an easier shot at it. If you have four or five or six good years in a row, you deserve it. Kaline should have been four or five years ago. It's a nice figure."

JULY 4

One of baseball's many untrue legends says that the team leading the league on the Fourth of July will win the pennant. It happens quite often, but not always. After finishing the four-game sweep of the Angels with a 13–10 victory this afternoon, the Tigers led the American League by eight and a half games over the Indians.

It was the largest lead on the Fourth in ten years.

Joe Sparma was behind, 4–0, by the second. But in the bottom of the inning the Tigers started the fireworks. Bill Freehan, Norm Cash and Willie Horton hit homers in a nine-run rally. Cash later hit another homer, and Jim Northrup hit two.

In four games with the Angels, the Tigers hit 13 home runs. Too bad they were leaving.

JULY 5

The A's and the Tigers were meeting for the first time since their brawl in May.

In the first inning Bill Freehan hit a three-run homer and the Tigers scored four times.

In the fourth inning Catfish Hunter hit Freehan with the pitch. It was the eleventh time Freehan had been hit by a pitched ball this year. He arose slowly and glared toward the mound, then trotted to first base.

In the fifth inning Freehan hit his second three-run homer of the game.

The Tigers won, 8–5, with Pat Dobson pitching excellent ball to save Mickey Lolich's victory. They had another five-game winning streak, the fifth in five weeks.

"I did not say anything toward the mound," said Freehan. "I said a prayer of thank you to the Lord."

Freehan was in a very hot streak of five home runs for the week and ten runs batted in during the past five games. A week before he had done nothing.

"I had zero for the week," he said. "It was a helluva week. I got hit four times and two walks.

"Well, I'm ahead of my pace of last year for getting hit. I might beat my twenty-one. I'm really not out to set a world's record.

"My view on the knockdown pitch is if the umpires don't fine guys, the batters are going to take things into their own hands. Somebody's going to break some pitcher's arm. They ought to fine them, not fifty dollars, but five hundred. I'm not trying to start a war, but Donny Wert has been hit in the head, Northrup was hit in the head, Willie's been hit in the head a couple of times.

"I'm a peace-loving guy, but what recourse does a batter have?

"I can't go out there. I'm the catcher, and we don't have anyone else."

JULY 6

Earl Wilson was struggling along today into the fifth inning. Then Rick Monday lashed the ball back at him. The ball cracked into Wilson's shoulder, then ricocheted off his jaw and onto his thumb. The triple blow felled Wilson. Don Wert picked up the spinning ball and fired it toward first. The throw was wild.

Wilson arose groggily and by instinct lurched over to back up third base. One batter later, Reggie Jackson lined the ball to the mound and it hit Wilson in his bare hand as he brought it up to cover himself.

Mayo Smith thereupon rescued Wilson from further battering. The A's won, 4–1, snapping the Tigers' five-game winning streak.

JULY 7

Joe Cronin, the president of the American League, called Mayo Smith. Cronin told Smith the American League was number one first with him, and Denny McLain had better be prepared for service in the All-Star game.

Up on the scoreboard before the doubleheader with the A's, Luis Tiant's number was flashed as the pitcher in Cleveland. The Tigers wondered if Cronin also had called Al Dark to ascertain Tiant's availability in the All-Star game.

"If Tiant pitches, McLain pitches," Denny said with resignation.

McLain pitched today's first game and yielded a 4–0 lead. Sal Bando and Reggie Jackson hit homers off him into the close-by outfield stands. It was 4–4 entering the bottom of the ninth. Lew Krausse, the A's pitcher, got Norm Cash on a line drive to second base for the first out in the ninth.

Krausse now had retired twelve Tigers in order. Bob Kennedy, the A's manager, walked to the mound anyway. He summoned Ed Sprague from the bullpen. Sprague was a right-handed sidearmer, and Kennedy wanted him to pitch to Willie Horton.

Sprague threw sidearm over the inside corner, right where Kennedy wanted the pitch. Horton lined the ball over the left-field fence.

It was Last Licks Victory Number Sixteen for the Tigers, as Willie ran into another of those mass celebrations at home plate. It was the fifth time he personally had won a game in the late innings.

The 5–4 victory was number sixteen for McLain, and he marched up to the third deck to watch the second game.

The press box is located on the third deck, and next to it is space for the radio and TV sportscasters. In this area is the organ Bill Fox plays between innings to soothe the customers.

Denny watched Joe Sparma pitch a couple of innings from there. Then he took Fox's place and serenaded his fans with a snappy version of "Satin Doll." The 36,000 customers never even realized they were being entertained by the winningest pitcher in the major leagues.

"What's the matter with the amplifier?" McLain asked Fox. "I'll send a man out to check it."

McLain was questioned about Tiant. Didn't he want to pitch in the All-Star game if the Indian pitcher did?

"I'm not competing with anybody in second place," said McLain. "I only compete out here."

He pointed down to the playing field at Tiger Stadium.

"I hope Tiant wins thirty, I hope he wins thirty-five—and finishes second, right where he is."

Sparma, booed as he warmed up, failed for the eleventh straight time to pitch a complete game. But the Tigers held off the A's, 7–6, to sweep the doubleheader. The A's scored three runs in the ninth. Then Mayo brought in Mickey Lolich for his first appearance in relief since the game in which the Tigers lost the pennant last October. Lolich caught Jackson on called strikes for the final out.

The Tigers went into the All-Star break with a nine-and-a-half-game lead over the Indians. The other contenders were sprawled further behind. Baltimore was ten and a half, Boston eleven and a half and Minnesota fifteen. The Red Sox had won eight straight ball games but could gain only one game. The Tigers won seven of eight at the same time.

"If we can play .500 the second half, we should be okay," said Smith as he headed to work as a coach at the All-Star game in Houston. "We're twenty-seven games over .500. I don't think we have to go fifty over. If we can get thirty over, that would be enough.

"The main thing in the second half is to avoid a prolonged losing streak. If we lose three, four, in a row and win two or three, we should be okay."

No league leader had been better off at the All-Star break for twenty-one years.

Tonight, fresh from his seventeenth victory, Denny McLain landed in Las Vegas aboard a borrowed Lear jet.

"I like Las Vegas," he said, and headed for the tables.

JULY 10

Denny McLain arrived in Houston for the All-Star game in the Astrodome, via Disneyland from Las Vegas.

In an unrelated event, the Las Vegas odds-makers announced they would take no more bets on the pennant race. The Tigers were too far ahead.

Luis Tiant started for the American League and gave up the only run of the game. McLain, despite his reluctance, pitched two scoreless innings.

After the game he reboarded the Lear jet and returned to Las Vegas.

JULY 16

The Tigers now only had to play .500 baseball. They had won 31 of their last 43 games before the break.

The starting pitching had been unreliable except for Mc-Lain. The hitting had been sporadic, but almost always the Tigers got the clutch hit when they needed one most. The bullpen had been more effective than last year but was beginning to strain.

The Tigers could be vulnerable. They were. They resumed their schedule on the road by losing four of the first five games after the All-Star game.

The Orioles unexpectedly fired Hank Bauer during the days off and hired Earl Weaver, a veteran minor league whip-cracker.

They promptly won five games and took second, cutting the Tigers' lead to six and a half games.

Out in Anaheim the Angels beat the Tigers twice. Bill Rigney sent the Tigers up to Oakland with a warning.

"Maybe the Tigers are starting to look over their shoulder," said the manager whose team had kept the Tigers from winning the pennant last year. "It looks like we might have a pennant race after all.

"The Tigers.have thirteen games to play with Baltimore. That could decide it all."

Only Denny McLain, lining up recording contracts and dates for his music group, could win a ball game.

His All-Star appearance caused Mayo Smith to postpone a start for McLain for one day. Mickey Lolich pitched the first game at Minnesota after the break. The Twins broke a six-game losing streak, 5–4, at the expense of the Tigers' bullpen. It was another last licks loss, and in it the Tigers squandered a two-run lead.

The next day the White Sox fired Eddie Stanky, and Mayo Smith called Al Lopez long distance to congratulate him on his second tour as manager of the White Sox.

McLain celebrated by pitching a three-hitter and beating the Twins, 5–1. He was 17–2 and his earned-run average was 1.98.

His victory was vital, again. It was the eighth time he had been a stopper—won a game after the previous one had been lost.

The Tigers then lost the next three games.

The bullpen twice blew leads in the final game at Minnesota. In the fourteenth inning the Tigers scored to break a 5–5 tie and had a chance for another last licks victory. But the Twins scored twice and won, 7–6. John Wyatt forced in the winning run by walking the other pitcher, Jim Roland, with the bases loaded.

The Tigers flew off to California on Saturday night and lost their next two games, 7–3 and 4–0.

There was a second crisis at Oakland. Not only were the Tigers looking over their shoulder, as Rigney had said, but they were guarding their clubhouse door.

They were expecting to be served the papers in the suit filed by the lady hit with the baseball during the last visit.

Mayo Smith made sure all the reporters' Baseball Writers Association cards were scrutinized before they entered the clubhouse.

Again Denny McLain stopped the Tigers from a prolonged losing streak. He beat the A's, 4–0, and his record was 18–2.

He started to smile at mention of $100,000 but rejected the statements about 30 victories with the usual, "I hope to win 19." He had nine straight victories.

Smith made another maneuver. He went against the rules and played Al Kaline at first base against a right-handed pitcher, Chuck Dobson. Kaline hit a home run.

JULY 18

Among them, Earl Wilson, Mickey Lolich and Joe Sparma had a combined record of 20–21. From Denny McLain's eighteen victories, the starting staff dropped to seven for the next two men. Lolich had seven and so did Sparma. But Sparma had lost nine games, including yesterday's 3–2 loss to the A's. He was taken out in the second, the twelfth straight time he was removed.

Mayo Smith was perturbed. Obviously McLain alone could not pitch the Tigers to the pennant. Not even if he did win thirty games.

Smith told Earl Wilson that so much depended on him today. Wilson won 22 games last year and was the Tigers' ace pitcher. Hurt twice this year and struggling, he had only 6 victories.

Wilson beat the A's, 3–1, and the Tigers were revived. They'd lost two and a half games of their lead on the road trip, but they were going home confident again.

They had a four-game series coming up with the Orioles. If they could halt the Orioles, there would be no more serious contenders. The Orioles, 6–2 since Earl Weaver became manager, thought of the series as important but not crucial.

"It's very important, but not a case of life and death," said Frank Robinson, their top hitter.

"I think this series is the first all year which we kind of have to build ourselves up for," said Brooks Robinson. "I think we're a better ball club than Detroit."

The Tigers flew across country tonight in a relieved atmosphere. Wilson had won an important ball game for them. No process server had penetrated their defenses in Oakland.

As the jet soared over the Rockies, Al Kaline stepped into the aisle and did an imitation of the long-haired popular singer Tiny Tim.

JULY 19

At the corner of Michigan and Trumbull, outside Tiger Stadium, a man furtively displayed two reserved seat tickets. The throngs pressed past him and somebody purchased the tickets at a premium. Never before had it been necessary for a ticket scalper to operate outside the ball park.

Tonight 53,208 people were in attendance, the Tigers' largest crowd in seven years. Jim Campbell ordered that no standing-room tickets be sold. His order was a precaution against another unruly scene. An estimated 5,000 people were unable to get into the park and went home to listen to Ernie Harwell and Ray Lane on the radio.

At the batting cage Mayo Smith was engrossed in watching Tommy Matchick, the scrawny redheaded shortstop who looks like a Huck Finn. With the Tigers again not hitting much, Smith, more or less, had appointed Matchick his shortstop. For the time being, anyway. Matchick was batting .225, which was higher than Ray Oyler and Dick Tracewski.

"Stop jerking your bat around so much," instructed Smith. "That gives you a tendency to swing at bad pitches. Just swing—don't go for the fences."

In the third, Frank Robinson hit a two-run homer off Mickey Lolich. In the sixth, Brooks Robinson lined a ball into left field and Willie Horton misjudged the ball and then made a diving catch. Suddenly Horton started writhing and upchucked the ball. Matchick picked it up and held Brooks to a double.

Horton was carried from the field on a stretcher. At the clubhouse it was determined he had pulled a muscle in his abdomen. In his dive for the ball, his protective cup had been forced upward and jammed him in the tummy.

The Orioles scored two more runs in the sixth and had a 4–0 lead. The Tigers didn't even have a hit yet off Wally Bunker, a right-hander just rejoining the Orioles from the International League.

Dick McAuliffe got the first hit with one out in the sixth, a two-run homer. Earl Weaver immediately yanked Bunker.

Baltimore led, 4–2, into the ninth. Pat Dobson got the Orioles out with difficulty. Don Buford started the inning with a double and was bunted to third. Dobson got Frank Robby on a pop-up to McAuliffe but walked Boog Powell. Then he forced Brooks Robby to ground out to McAuliffe.

Jim Northrup singled in the bottom of the ninth for the Tigers' third hit. Al Kaline walked, and up popped Weaver to lift Eddie Watt. He brought in lefty John O'Donoghue to face Norm Cash.

This was a bunt situation, and Cash rolled one toward third base. Brooks Robinson made a sensational play and forced Kaline at second.

Weaver popped out of the dugout again. He brought in Moe Drabowsky, his most dependable reliever, to pitch to Bill Freehan. Freehan was only 5 for 34 since the All-Star game. He forced Cash at second.

Drabowsky stayed to face the next batter, Matchick. In all his appearances this year, Drabowsky had permitted only one home run.

Now he was one strike away from victory.

Matchick swung and hit the 3–2 pitch into the overhang of the upper right-field seats for a game-winning three-run homer.

Clapping his hands, Matchick ran around the bases and into the mass of teammates at home plate. The Orioles, beaten 5–4 in a game they had almost won, walked off the field in shock.

The large crowd was in the same shock. This time certainly their team had been licked.

Usually after a ball game the corridor from the press elevator to the clubhouse is jammed. You have to fight and shove your way to the door. Ribs are elbowed.

Tonight, despite the huge crowd, the passageway was almost empty and the writers could dash. The few people walking beneath the stands looked stupefied or wore bemused smiles. Most of the crowd remained transfixed in the seats.

"They all stayed," said Northrup in the clubhouse. "They kept sitting in the stands after it was over. I never saw anything like it."

"Routine," said Al Kaline.

"I remembered what Mayo said all through the game," said Tom Matchick. "In the situation, I was just looking for a ball I could pull."

"Well, I started thinking we'd won a lot of these games in the first half," said Jim Campbell in a confession that he had given up on this game.

"They're dying for a pennant here," said Matchick. "They want a pennant."

"If you weren't so ugly, I'd kiss you," said McAuliffe to Matchick.

"Why do we win so many games like this?" said Mayo Smith of Last Licks Victory Number Seventen. "They believe in each other. If one can't do it, the next one will. Faith, they have faith in each other."

"Your club was down, wasn't it?" somebody said to Smith.

"We weren't down," said Smith, contorting. "How can you look good when you're not hitting the ball? We weren't down or flat.

"Now listen to me. There's no way you're going through an entire season at the pace we started off.

"But a dramatic victory like this has to pick you up a little more. Especially the first game of a series."

The Tigers had knocked the Orioles eight and a half games back, and the Indians again were in second, seven and a half behind. It couldn't be much better, particularly with Denny McLain pitching tomorrow.

JULY 20

Denny McLain at the organ with his combo had a new contract with Capitol Records.

McLain had won nine games in a row, and the Orioles were the only team to escape him this year. Dave McNally pitched against him as he sought his nineteenth victory today.

In the fifth inning McNally hit a home run off McLain. McNally had not gotten a hit before this season, in 40 at-bats. In the same inning, Frank Robinson hit a home run.

Mayo Smith took McLain out with the Tigers losing, 5–0. They lost the game, 5–3.

"He's not that bad a hitter," said McLain when told of McNally's previous futility.

"I could have hit that pitch.

"Frank Robinson—he thinks he's God's gift to baseball. That's the first home run he's ever hit off me.

"Robinson, he's not tough. But he's got to be tougher than me. Why? Because he's making a hundred thousand dollars, that's why.

"Funny, I've lost three games and all of them have been here. Funny, I've won every game I've started on the road. I hate to pitch in this ———— place. It's not the fans, no, it's the fences. I wish we could take our own fans to Washington or some place.

"I still like my chances to win nineteen. I might have three starts left this month. What month are we in?

"I'm going to pitch against Baltimore again next week and it might mean something."

If it worked right, Denny McLain could be pitching against the Orioles for his twentieth victory.

JULY 21

Boo . . . boo . . . boo . . .

More than 48,000 infidels attended today's doubleheader. The Orioles, stunned two days ago, won both games, 5–2 and 4–1.

They danced off the field, five and a half games behind the Tigers—five games closer than they were ten days ago. The Indians also were five and a half out, and the fans were beginning to think of their twenty-three years without a pennant.

The Tigers were a team reputed to fold under stress. They had done this so often in other years. So the fans booed them and feared for them.

Only Tom Matchick did any hitting—and without his home run Friday night the lead would be three and a half games now.

They had only ten hits in the doubleheader. And without hitting, the burden was too much for the pitchers. Both Earl Wilson and Pat Dobson, replacing Joe Sparma in the rotation, were knocked out.

The Tigers sat in their clubhouse after their first doubleheader loss eating fried chicken in silence.

"This might be the best thing that happened to us," said Al Kaline. "It'll shake us up a bit. It may shake me up. Every year there's a crisis—and this is our crisis."

In the second game Kaline played left field. The Tigers loaded the bases in the first inning with none out. Then Kaline popped up and the Tigers got only one run—their only run—out of the situation.

"When you only score three runs in two games in this ball park, you're going to get your butt beat," said Mayo Smith.

Pitching coach Johnny Sain, right, had a hand in Denny McLain's development.

"I'd like to have had somebody tell me at the start of the season I'd be five and a half games up at this time. I'd have taken that. A lot of them need rest now."

Outside Mayo's office a tall Arkansas philosopher dressed slowly. John Sain was the pitching coach, a quiet man who was credited with much of the making of Denny McLain. Sain once had pitched for the Boston Braves and beat Bobby Feller in the World Series. He had been in other World Series later on.

"I've been on eight pennant winners." said Sain, "and so far this club has had less trouble than any of them."

From their first doubleheader loss the Tigers went directly

to Cooperstown. They were to play in the annual Hall of Fame exhibition game and continue on to Washington and Baltimore.

JULY 23

The Tigers were in danger because Mayo Smith went to Denny McLain and asked him to pitch again on short rest. He pitched tonight three days after his last start—with two days' rest, as they say in the dugout. Twice before, in the surge of June and July, Smith had asked McLain to pitch with two days' rest. McLain did and won both times.

Tonight he had trouble with the weak Senators and was behind, 4–3, in the eighth. It could have been tied except for some dawdling on the base paths. Jim Northrup jogged toward home on Bill Freehan's single. But Al Kaline was out trying to go from first to third on the hit. It was the third out of the inning, and because Northrup had not yet reached home, an apparent run was nullified.

This was the first event that ired Smith. Then a disputed hit-batsman and a couple of pop hits in the Senators' three-run rally in the sixth made him angrier.

So McLain was a run behind in the eighth and Smith would again be forced to pinch-hit for him. That was the projection as the Tigers went to bat.

Kaline walked, and with the short fence in D.C. Stadium, Smith wanted Willie Horton to swing for a home run.

Horton laid down one of the best bunts Smith ever saw—only it was not really a sacrifice situation. Smith's face turned red and he stomped his shoe on the dugout steps. It was a wasted out, really.

Freehan walked and Smith went to his pinch hitters. Jim

Detroit Tigers

Gates Brown

Price singled in Kaline with the tying run. Norm Cash tried to check his swing and popped out for the second out.

Gates Brown was the third straight pinch batter. Brown was the Tigers' celebrated pinch hitter. Retained because nobody else would take him, Brown had become a priceless object because of his clutch hits. He'd hit safely nine times in sixteen pinch appearances.

Now he batted for McLain and singled to right for his tenth pinch hit. But he hit the ball too hard, and Cap Peterson's throw beat Freehan to the plate. But Paul Casanova, the catcher, dropped the ball, and Freehan slid in safely. The Tigers were ahead—and McLain had won another game which he had left as the apparent losing pitcher.

The 6–4 victory, protected by Jon Warden's relief work in the ninth, put McLain within one of a 20-game season. July had a week to go and McLain was already 19–3.

For the twenty-seventh time the Tigers pulled a game out with a rally in the seventh or later. This was one of the most important of the twenty-seven.

"We were lucky," said Smith. "Maybe we needed a game like this to turn us around."

McLain, for the first time, was hinting around to friends about the possibility of winning 30 games. He didn't quite say it, but: "If it means anything, on the last day of the season I'll pitch"—and you realized what he meant.

"I'd like a little rest before the World Series, but if it means anything, well . . ."

Since the subject was mentioned, the name of Bob Gibson was offered. "Would you like to pitch against him?"

"I'd like to pitch against Gibson in the World Series, even if it was in Kalamazoo," said Denny McLain.

McLain was the stopper again, for the tenth time—and again a losing streak longer than three games was forestalled.

JULY 25

"We're in a rut," said Mayo Smith.

The Tigers couldn't get another winning streak started either. Mickey Lolich lost again last night at Washington, 6–3. He had a two-run lead and got racked.

Smith was groping for a pitcher and decided to bring Joe Sparma back from exile tonight.

Sparma pitched his first complete game in two months, although rain cut it short to six and a half innings. But he beat the Senators, 4–1, and gave up only a single to Paul Casanova. Jim Northrup hit two homers.

The Tigers took the bus up to Baltimore for a three-game weekend series. The Orioles, idle tonight, were five and a half games behind. The Tigers were weakened by the departure of Tom Matchick for two weeks' duty in the National Guard.

JULY 26

Baltimore is an apathetic baseball town. The Orioles had created an American League pennant race, and there was some stirred-up interest. More than 35,000 turned out tonight for the first of the three-game series with the Tigers. Yet there were lots of good seats available in Memorial Stadium that would have been occupied for any pro football game involving the Colts.

The bullpen was causing Mayo Smith some worry; the young arms had lost some effectiveness. Earlier today the Tigers acquired Don McMahon, a well-journeyed right-hander, from the White Sox for Dennis Ribant. The Tigers were obtaining a thirty-eight-year-old for a twenty-six-year-old. But McMahon had relieved in the tension of pennant races before.

Young Daryl Patterson, for example, never had. Until tonight.

Earl Wilson started against the Orioles, a team he usually defeats. Wilson had a 2–0 lead in the sixth when he strained his left knee. It was the third time he had been hurt this season, and Smith replaced him with Jon Warden. Wilson left with a runner on and a 2–0 count on Frank Robinson. Warden walked him, and Boog Powell bunted and got a single on it.

The Orioles had the bases loaded with none out, and Smith went to his bullpen again. The gangling Patterson was called into this very difficult situation.

Patterson struck out Fred Valentine, a switch-batter.

He struck out Brooks Robinson.

He struck out Davey Johnson.

The Orioles left three runners on the bases and still trailed, 2–0.

Patterson pitched the rest of the ball game and gave up one hit in his four innings.

The Tigers won, 4–1, and it was a critically important victory, credited to Wilson. The lead was raised to six and a half games.

JULY 27

Over the past forty-eight years only one pitcher had become a 20-game winner while the baseball season was still in July. That pitcher was Bob (Lefty) Grove, of the Athletics, in 1931—the year he won 31 games.

Denny McLain tonight beat the Orioles, 9–0, with a three-hitter and became a 20-game winner in July.

The Tigers might not hit much for the other pitchers, but they hit for McLain. Tonight Willie Horton hit two homers and Dick McAuliffe, Don Wert and Al Kaline each hit one.

Kaline was back in right field for the first time since his arm had been broken, as Mayo Smith changed his outfield array. Mickey Stanley was rested, and Norm Cash played and had four hits.

When the game ended, McLain jumped joyously off the mound and pounded his fist into his glove. In the clubhouse he stuffed a cigar into his mouth and posed with it.

He talked of the Detroit newspaper strike, now eight and a half months old, and of the smoke bomb that had been in his car.

"The big thing is the writers are not around demoralizing the players," said McLain.

He talked of the recent cover piece in *Sports Illustrated*, which characterized him as Mighty Mouth.

"They made me look flamboyant," he said. "Mr. Party Boy of 1968. They hurt my image."

Denny McLain was ebullient.

"If I were three and twenty, I wouldn't be in Detroit," he said. "Everybody loves a winner."

McLain thought about how difficult it had been to win 20 two years ago, the year he had 13 at midseason.

"It took three shots to win number twenty," he said. "I've been lucky this year. I haven't been hung up on any number yet.

"Knock on wood."

McLain reached for the steel wire wall of his locker and knocked it. Then he tapped a table, a wooden one.

Rick Ferrell, a vice-president of the Tigers, was involved in the Tigers' acquisition of McLain from the White Sox four years before.

The legend is that the White Sox could keep only two of

A winning battery: Denny McLain and catcher Bill Freehan.

three bonus pitchers. They decided to match two of them, McLain and Bruce Howard, in an intra squad game. Howard's team won, 2–1, and the White Sox put McLain on first-year waivers.

The story isn't entirely accurate, but it enhances the McLain mystique. Anyway the Tigers claimed him.

"It was the best waiver deal in history," Ferrell said. "We paid eight thousand dollars for him."

The Tigers were safe again, seven and a half games in front of the Orioles.

JULY 28

Mickey Lolich had not won a game for more than three weeks, and Mayo Smith was giving him another try.

But the Orioles pounded seven hits off him in an inning and one-third, and Smith yanked him from the game.

Dave McNally held the Tigers to three hits and won, 5–1. Willie Horton provided the only run, a home run with two outs and two strikes on him in the ninth.

"I'm going to take Lolich out of the rotation for a while," said Smith. "He has not been good in his last three outs. He's going to the bullpen."

JULY 30

Earl Wilson put a harness over his sore left knee and went out to pitch against the Yankees tonight. He hit a home run and won, 5–0.

The victory gave the Tigers a split in the two-game series —sufficient under Mayo Smith's formula. Last night the Tigers managed only five hits and Joe Sparma was the loser as the Yankees won, 7–2.

After tonight's game Wilson sat in the clubhouse and stuck his elbow in a bucket of ice.

"I didn't hurt anything tonight," he said.

JULY 31

It was raining torrents at Tiger Stadium, but 37,000 were in the place, so the management waited and waited.

"It's going to rain all night, Mac," said Denny McLain to Dick McAuliffe.

"I think so," said Mac. "I'm going to take my uniform off."

McLain sat in the dugout in the half-dark ball park and propped his feet against a cement post.

He looked at a schedule.

"I'll start here, and here, and here, and here," he said, pointing to specific dates on the orange-printed card.

In his mind he was calculating just about when he would win number thirty.

Already people were wondering about the wisdom of a confrontation between McLain and Bob Gibson when—if— the Tigers and Cardinals played in the World Series.

"If I give up a run, he'll win," said McLain as the rain continued to fall. "If he gives up a run, I'll win."

He laughed.

"Really, it'll be one to nothing, two to one, something like that.

"I want to pitch the first game."

The players wondered if the game would be postponed.

Malcolm W. Emmons

Dick McAuliffe

"Anybody know where I can buy another arm?" said Mc-Lain. "I hope it keeps raining. My arm's tired, sore. It feels like a thud. I can do everything with it, but I know it's there."

The rain stopped and Jess Walls' grounds keepers fixed up the field.

Dick McAuliffe put his uniform back on. McLain, disappointed, went out to warm up.

McAuliffe hit a double his first time up, then a home run, then a single, then another double. He was four for four, and he got all four hits off a left-hander, Frank Bertaina. Mac is not supposed to hit that well against left-handers.

"I'm hitting them better than ever before," he said. "Bertaina's not an overpowering left-hander. To me you can put him in the right-hander's category because of that."

Denny McLain, who had not wanted to pitch, pitched a shutout and gave up four hits. It was his twenty-first victory against three losses, and the score was 4–0.

"It's been a long time since I threw a shutout in this park," he said. "I hate this park, I hate this park, I hate this park."

It had been more than a year.

This afternoon a new prototype organ had been delivered to McLain's home.

"I'm going with Hammond this year and they gave me an X-77," he said. "It costs fifty-five hundred dollars. I'm going to introduce it in New York the nineteenth of August.

"Oh, yes, we'll open up in Las Vegas the nineteenth of October. Spread the word. At the Riviera. The Series starts the second.

"And next week we'll be recording three days for Capitol. The album will be called 'Denny McLain at the Organ.'"

"You sound a little money-hungry, Denny," said a listener.

"No, I'm not money-hungry," said McLain. "Right, I'm money-hungry."

The Tigers finished July with a seven-game lead over the Orioles.

AUGUST 2

Mayo Smith shuddered and you could hear the ice cubes tinkle.

"That was the toughest game I ever managed in my life," he said.

The Tigers were at Minnesota. They had lost the final game of the series with Washington back home, 9–3. Mayo had another dispute with an umpire, Nestor Chylak, about a home run that went out on the wrong side of the foul pole but was decreed good. That hurt the Tigers.

Pat Dobson was bombed out as the starter, and the bullpen was not effective.

It was an interesting week for Ron Hansen, the Senators' shortstop. He made a triple play over at Cleveland, then crushed the Tigers with a grand slam home run. Then he was traded today to the White Sox.

Now tonight, Mayo was forced to scramble—which is to maneuver under stress. The Tigers scored four times in the first against the Twins.

But Joe Sparma, the starter, and Mickey Lolich, in bullpen exile, could not retain the lead. The Twins were ahead, 5–4, by the fourth.

In the fifth, with two outs, Mickey Stanley, Al Kaline, Willie Horton and Bill Freehan singled for two runs.

Smith brought in thirty-eight-year-old Don McMahon to preserve the lead. McMahon pitched into the ninth and the Tigers still led, shakily, 6–5.

Then there was trouble. Cesar Tovar hit a pop-up near the mound and it fell between Dick McAuliffe and Dick Tracewski. John Hiller came in and prevented Rich Reese from bunting and got him on a liner to Don Wert. Wert stabbed the ball and doubled Tovar at first. Ted Uhlaender singled to short. Smith brought in lanky Daryl Patterson.

Patterson, after a battle, caught Bob Allison on strikes, and Mayo vaulted from the dugout, his fist high in triumph.

The Tigers had kept the Orioles from chopping a game off their six-game lead.

AUGUST 4

Denny McLain again was the stopper today, for the eleventh time. He beat the Twins, 2–1, for his twenty-second victory.

What he did this time was important because for three games the Tigers' starting pitchers had not been able to survive through the third inning.

Yesterday the Twins had defeated Earl Wilson in a 4–0 game.

McLain now had started 15 times on the road, and his record there was 15–0.

Even so, the Tigers were forced by the schedule to go home. Ahead were two unbroken weeks of competition against the Indians and Red Sox—14 straight games against opposition still regarded as dangerous.

The Orioles were second, five and a half behind. After them were the Indians, eight and a half behind, and the Red Sox, nine and a half out.

The Tigers were in a position to be damaged.

AUGUST 6

A twi-night doubleheader is something artificial. The first game begins in bright sunshine—with the arc lights turned on. The shadows of the grandstands lengthen on the field. The lights are on to help day blend into night without much change in illumination.

The habit in Detroit is for the people to show up midway through the first game when a twi-nighter is scheduled. They get out of the factories and offices, drive home, have dinner and take the kids downtown for a ball game and a half.

Tonight 48,413 people were in Tiger Stadium at one time or another watching baseball.

Most of them did not see John Hiller strike out the first six Indians to face him in the first game. Six straight at the start of a game was a major league record. Back in 1912, Walter Johnson became the first to strike out the first five batters in a game. But nobody, until late this afternoon, had struck the first six.

As impressive as his record was, Hiller still trailed the Indians, 1–0, in the eighth inning. Luis Tiant was Cleveland's pitcher, and his record was 17–7. He had eight shutouts and was within five outs of another.

Then Don Wert, who had been hit in the head by another Indian player in June, came up. He had got only 14 hits in 102 at-bats since he returned from the hospital. Tiant, a man of many motions, pitched sidearm, up tight. Wert swung at the pitch and lined it into the lower left-field seats.

The score was 1–1 after eight. It stayed 1–1 through the ninth, tenth, eleventh, twelfth, thirteen, fourteenth, fifteenth and sixteenth innings.

Mayo Smith employed five men from his bullpen, Mickey Lolich included, through the innings of runlessness. Alvin

Dark used three men, only because he had a pitching shortage.

In the eleventh the Indians were very close to scoring but did not. They failed in later chances in the fifteenth and sixteenth.

The Tigers had a chance in the twelfth, but Al Kaline and Willie Horton couldn't get the hit. In the fifteenth, Kaline again stranded a runner in scoring position. In the sixteenth, Norm Cash struck out with the bases filled.

In the seventeenth, Horton singled off Mike Paul, and Bill Freehan, for the sixteenth time, was hit by a pitch. Mayo Smith signaled a bunt, but Wert forced Horton at third with it.

Dick Tracewski came to the plate with a record of 1 hit in his previous 32 at-bats. Four hours and 28 minutes after the game had started in sunshine, Tracewski lined a single into right center and Freehan scored the winning run.

Last Licks Victory Number Eighteen, by a 2–1 score, caused another spontaneous celebration among the players at home plate.

It was 10 P.M., and this was Shrine Night. It meant 45 minutes between games and a parade of colorfully costumed Shriners, and horses, and a man in a fez swinging a scimitar.

Upstairs in the press box Ed Browalski, the writer from the *Polish Daily News*, was savoring the winning hit by Tracewski.

"They never had a parade like this for any other guy," Browalski told his colleagues.

It took almost a month, but the Tigers finally had evened their record at .500 for the games after the All-Star break.

Joe Sparma, booed, started the second game. In the second inning Cash came to the plate, and he too was heavily booed for his misdeed in the sixteenth inning of the first game.

Cash whacked the ball into the right-field stands. He pranced around the bases, touched home and seemed to yell something to the fans in the third-base seats. In a corner of the dugout a teammate interrupted the cheering to jerk his right arm upward in an undignified gesture. Mayo Smith immediately spoke to the culprit.

In the fourth inning Sparma surrendered two runs and Smith yanked him. Lolich came in and pitched better than he had in a month. Gates Brown started a four-run rally in the sixth, and Kaline, booed, drove in two of those with a pinch double.

At one o'clock in the morning, with eight innings completed, the league curfew caused the game to be suspended with the Tigers ahead, 5–2. It would be finished tomorrow night.

Lolich, who had been without a victory for a month and a day, was impatient. He was only 7–7. He went over to John Sain, his pitching coach.

"Have you ever been a half-game over .500?" inquired Lolich, the motorcycle driver.

In the wee hours Smith dressed rapidly.

"We had our hitting and pitching slump at the same time," he said, as though it had now gone.

"Then you've had your lull?" asked a reporter.

"As long as our bullpen holds up, we've had," he said. "We got twelve scoreless innings from them tonight.

"Sparma's going to the bullpen. Lolich pitched well for the first time in a long time, but he's staying in the bullpen.

"I'll probably use Dobson and Patterson as starters this weekend against Boston. I've held off a long time taking people out of the bullpen. It's nut-cuttin' time now, so we've got to throw the shovel with the ———.

"I don't say take Sparma and Lolich out and shoot them. They could come back."

AUGUST 7

John Wyatt needed four minutes to retire the Indians in the ninth inning of last night's suspended game.

Mayo Smith rested Dick McAuliffe and Jim Northrup, despite his five straight hits last night, in the regular game. He lined up nine right-handed batters against Sam McDowell.

The Tigers' first started with Mickey Stanley getting a hit on a roller to third and Dick Tracewski walking. McDowell threw a ball to Al Kaline.

Al Dark walked to the mound and took McDowell out.

"He asked me, 'Is that all the harder you can throw?'" said suddenly removed Sam.

Earl Wilson won the ball game, 6–1, with Daryl Patterson's relief work. Willie Horton hit his twenty-seventh home run. Dave Campbell, the rookie brought up with Tom Matchick in the Army, hit his first—his first big league hit. Campbell was the Tigers' fourth second baseman of the year. He played the game with a 101-degree fever.

"McDowell was out at eleven last night," said Mayo Smith later in the Tigers' clubhouse.

How did he know?

"I have my spies," said Smith. "Maybe that hurt his elbow."

There was another brushback incident. Hal Kurtz, the right-hander whose pitch had beaned Don Wert in June, twice dropped Horton with close pitches.

Horton arose and said something to plate umpire Marty Springstead—Marvelous Marty, as Mayo called him.

"I'll tell you when he's wild," said Springstead, according to Horton's reconstruction of the conversation.

"Will you take care of my family when he hits me?" asked Willie.

During the ball game a foul bounced out of the left-field seats. Willie retrieved it and tossed it back to his followers.

"You've got to have fun in this game," said Horton. "If you don't have fun, it's not worth a damn."

The Tigers were having fun with their winning streak four games and the Orioles six games back.

AUGUST 8

The newspapers were coming back, the nine-month strike was over.

"When we have player meetings now, we sit around and interview one another," Mayo Smith had been saying all year. "That's so when the writers come back, we won't be out of practice."

The *News* and *Free Press* were returning with the Tigers in another five-game winning streak.

Denny McLain won his twenty-third tonight. He beat the Indians, 13–1, on another night when rain could have postponed the game—had the management not waited and waited. Bill Freehan socked two home runs.

"We cut five sides of our album today," said Denny the maestro. "We cut one eighteen times and finally got it and then missed the last chord. So I threw the whole piece out."

McLain was 23–3.

"You know, when I didn't get a decision in my first two starts, I predicted I'd be 0–0 for the year," he said.

"I have to go to South Bend tomorrow for a clothes endorsement."

He opened an envelope from an ad agency.

"I've got so many I can't handle them," he said.

"You've got until March one," said a newly working writer.

"You might not see me in Lakeland on March the first. Strange things happen. No, I don't mean I'll be traded."

McLain grabbed the change pocket of his trousers.

"You know what I mean—if I win thirty and don't get two hundred thousand, I might not be there. Two hundred thousand dollars."

This was double the figure everybody was mentioning, and McLain had that facetious grin on his Irish face.

The Tigers had scrubbed the Indians from third place by sweeping the four-game series. Dick Tracewski had turned on the Indians for the second time, this time dropping them from the race. They were twelve and one-half games back—and the Red Sox had taken over third as they flew to Detroit.

For the sixth time, the Tigers had a five-game winning streak.

AUGUST 9

Mayo Smith did not always make the perfect move. Tonight with Red Sox on second and third and two out, Smith made the correct, game-proven decision. He told John Wyatt, the relief pitcher, to walk Reggie Smith intentionally. Joe Foy, the next hitter, hit a grand slam home run and the Red Sox won the first game of the series, 5–3.

Dick Tracewski hit another home run for the Tigers, his fourth, and that matched the previous total in his career. Gates Brown got another pinch hit, a homer, and was 16 out of 26, a .577 average, strictly as a pinch hitter.

"You forget the ones you win like that," said Mayo Smith of the late-inning loss.

And the Orioles again were five and one-half games behind. The Red Sox, too, were getting a bit closer, nine games back.

AUGUST 10

A little after ten this morning Mickey Lolich, the relief pitcher, put on his crash helmet. He then boarded one of his five Kawasaki motorcycles and roared from the driveway of his home in Washington, about 20 miles from Detroit.

Hunched forward on the seat, peering through the plastic bubble, Lolich drove toward downtown. It was about eleven when he ground to a halt in the green-walled parking compound at Tiger Stadium.

He walked to his locker, which is the first one on the right in the Tigers' clubhouse, and sat down to read some mail. Most of the correspondents were critical.

"Some of these accuse me of not trying," said Lolich. "Baseball's my living and I've got a family to support. How can I not try?"

Lolich was unhappy at the loss of his job in the Tigers' starting rotation. He would go out to the bullpen and probably sit in the subterranean, screened-in dugout where the relievers wait to be beckoned. The sun would glare off the concrete roof and he would bake inside.

Daryl Patterson was liberated from the bullpen to start today.

He left in the fifth with the Red Sox ahead, 3–1. The Tigers scored a run in the sixth and another in the seventh on Mickey Stanley's single. That tied it, 3-all.

Norm Cash had been booed today, as normal, by the crowd which went above 44,000 on Ladies Day.

In the eighth he dropped a throw at first base, and the runner eventually reached third with another on first. With one out, Mayo Smith made another of several treks to the mound.

Lolich was out of the dugout and warming up. Mayo Smith

signaled his left arm although George Scott, the next hitter, batted right. Lolich became the Tigers' sixth pitcher of the day.

Scott struck out on Lolich's first three pitches. Lolich then got Jerry Adair on a fly to right.

Leading off the Tigers' eighth, Cash cracked a drive into the right-field stands for a 4–3 lead. It was his third hit and he received an ovation.

Lolich went out for the ninth. He quickly retired Mike Andrews and Dalton Jones. Carl Yastrzemski singled. But Lolich retired Ken Harrelson to win the game, 4–3.

It was his second victory in the few days he had been banished to the bullpen.

"He's throwing the way he did last September, when he was the best pitcher in baseball," said John Sain, the taciturn pitching coach.

This was Last Licks Victory Number Nineteen.

Lolich reboarded his cycle and roared into the early sunlit evening for the 20-mile ride back home.

AUGUST 11

At Metropolitan Airport a cashier at the parking lot leaned into his booth to catch Ernie Harwell's message on his transistor. The man broke into a bad-toothed grin and said: "He did it again, he did it again."

The Tigers signed Gates Brown out of a prison in Ohio. Gates was in on a breaking and entering charge. Pat Mullin, the old outfielder who was scouting for the Tigers, went down there, and Gates hit a couple of balls over the wall. The Tigers offered him $7,000, and he accepted it and was paroled. That was nine years ago.

"I'm resigned to the fact that I just ain't going to play," said Brown, who'd hit a pinch homer in his first big league at-bat.

There was no room in the Tigers' outfield for Gates. As a second thought last April, when he provided their first last licks victory, the Tigers found room on their bench.

There were two games today with the Red Sox, and 49,000 people turned out to see them.

The Red Sox scored four times off Earl Wilson in the first inning of the opener. Dalton Jones hit a two-run homer and then Joe Foy hit one, too.

The Tigers got a run back in the third, another in the sixth, another in the seventh and another in the eighth to tie it. Bill Freehan hit a homer, and Wayne Comer hit the first of his career.

Mickey Lolich came in again in relief in the tenth. He escaped in the twelfth by getting Carl Yastrzemski on a double play with two runners on base. He escaped in the thirteenth by getting Rico Petrocelli with three runners on base.

With two outs in the bottom of the fourteenth and the first game 4 hours, 23 minutes old, Brown batted for Lolich.

Brown cracked the ball into the lower right-field stands for his sixteenth hit—the fourth game-winner—in 27 pinch-hit at-bats.

The 5–4 victory was Lolich's third in five days as a relief pitcher. He pitched scoreless baseball the last five innings until the game was won for him.

Mayo Smith rewarded Brown by putting him into left field for the second game.

John Hiller opposed Gary Bell in a scoreless game until the seventh. Then Reggie Smith put the Red Sox two runs up in the seventh with a home run.

The Tigers, in their fashion, tied it in the bottom of the eighth, Norm Cash driving in both runs with a single.

But the Red Sox crushed the Tigers with three runs in the top of the ninth for a 5–2 lead. Reggie Smith hit another homer. Then the Red Sox scored twice more off Jon Warden, winless and little used since early season.

It was nearing nine o'clock, and the Red Sox's outburst in the ninth caused half the crowd to rush for the expressway.

The bottom of the ninth started with Jim Price coaxing a walk from Bell. Wayne Comer flied to left for the first out. Bill Freehan batted for Warden and hit a soft blooper over shortstop for a single. Lefty Bill Landis came in to pitch to Dick McAuliffe. Mac dribbled a ball between first and second, and Price scored to make it 5–3. Jerry Stephenson came in to pitch to Mickey Stanley.

Stanley bounced the ball back toward the pitcher. The ball bounced high and over the mound toward second base. It eluded two groping gloves and went into short center. Freehan scored to make it 5–4.

Al Kaline now was the batter. He had two strikes on him and then jabbed the ball off the end of his bat. The ball blooped over second baseman Mike Andrews, who couldn't quite grab it with his glove.

Mac scored, and the game suddenly, through an assault of putt-putt hits, was tied, 5–5. Stanley ran to third.

Brown was the next batter, and Dick Williams brought in a left-hander, Sparky Lyle, to pitch. Gates had batted but once all season against a left-hander.

He looked over to the dugout. Mayo Smith kept looking right back at him.

"Don't expect a fastball from Lyle," said Cash, who was headed to the on-deck circle.

All Brown expected was a pinch hitter for him. Williams brought the Red Sox in to make a possible play on Stanley at the plate.

Lyle threw a slider, and Brown nudged the ball toward the first baseman, George Scott. The ball rolled and squibbed, and Scott reached across frantically for it. But the ball kept bouncing right past him—the fifth consecutive poorly hit single.

Stanley came scooting in from third base with the winning

run, 6–5. At second base Gates Brown was mobbed by his teammates.

He had accounted for Last Licks Victories Numbers Twenty and Twenty-one on the same day.

"If this sounds boastful, I don't mean it to," said Gates Brown. "I just think I hit better when we need it.

"Man, I was scared all day."

Gates sat in the clubhouse laughing.

"Hey, I wonder what all those fans that went home must be thinking now," he said. "They must be madder than hell."

And so the Tigers now had brushed off the Red Sox, too. The reigning league champions were shoved—hard—12 games behind. And the Orioles lost, too, dropping seven games back in second place.

The Tigers took seven out of the eight games from the Indians and Red Sox in the two series. Now they had to play them in successive series again on the road.

AUGUST 14

Denny McLain won number twenty-four for the first night in Cleveland, 6–3.

Time and *Life* were moved in with him now, recording his every statement, probing his life from infancy. Ed Sullivan and Joey Bishop wanted him for their shows. He already was set for a spot on the *Today Show* and for an organ recital next week in New York at the Hampshire House.

Much was contingent on Denny's hitting 30, and for the first time, he admitted to an audience he had been stuck on the number.

"Of course, I'm thinking about thirty victories," he said

after number twenty-four. "I've been shooting for thirty ever since I won my fifteenth."

Last night Cleveland's Sonny Siebert shut out the Tigers on three hits, 1–0. That broke their four-game winning streak.

Mayo Smith took Joe Sparma out of the bullpen to pitch against the Indians tonight.

In the bottom of the first, Sparma walked Lee Maye, the second batter. In the bullpen Mickey Lolich started to warm up.

Bill Freehan gave the Tigers a 1–0 lead in the second with a home run off Luis Tiant, the 18-game winner.

In the second, Lolich again started to warm up. Sparma again retired the Indians without a run.

In the third, Lolich warmed up when two Indians reached base. But Sparma again got out of the inning with the 1–0 lead.

In the fourth, Azcue singled hard. Lolich started to warm up again. Max Alvis walked and Smith walked to the mound. He signaled for Lolich.

Sparma walked to the dugout and threw his glove. He waved his arms and went to the clubhouse.

Lolich finished the shutout for his fourth relief victory in eight days, 3–0.

Sparma was still furious about being taken out with a 1–0 lead in the fourth inning. He was further enraged over a relief pitcher warming in the first inning after he walked one batter.

"I can't be concerned about his feelings," said Smith. "We've got to win. I only wanted Joe to pitch the first few innings, and he did that job for us."

That did not soothe Sparma very much.

AUGUST 15

Charley Creedon, the traveling secretary, kindly arranged for the Tigers to get a good night of sleep before today's flight to Boston. As he boarded the jet charter at Cleveland's Hopkins Airport, Joe Sparma still was upset. His anger had not diminished. He believed Mayo Smith had humiliated him.

Sparma did not veil his feelings when he unloaded to Detroit's two sports columnists, Pete Waldmeir of the *News* and Joe Falls of the *Free Press*.

"What kind of man does he think I am?

"He could have called me and explained. A man needs his pride. If you take his pride away in front of his teammates, what has he got left?

"I'm not saying Mayo's a bad manager.

"But a man has got to draw the line someplace, and I'm drawing it. Mayo hasn't played any favorites. He's been patient with my pitching, I suppose. But I honestly don't know if I'll be able to play for him any more. Sure, we won the game. And that's supposed to be everything.

"Afterwards, Mayo sent another player to me—one of the older players—to tell me that personal records don't count—after all, it's the team. The player explained, too, about the strategy with me and Lolich, about having Cleveland load up with right-handed hitters against me and then bring in a left-hander.

"My gripe is why didn't Mayo tell me before the game?

"Mayo had to treat me like a man and he didn't," Sparma told Falls as the Tigers' plane flew across New York State toward Boston. "If that's all the confidence he had in me, why did he start me in the first place?

"Hell, Woody Hayes never treated me that way."

When the plane landed in Boston, Sparma drove up to Gloucester to visit a friend.

He thought about what he had said and the reaction back home. He thought that the Tigers' wives would be having a get-together tonight and what Connie would think when they turned on the television. He thought what the other wives would think when they heard what he had said and how they would look at Connie.

Sparma telephoned home and told Mrs. Sparma to be prepared.

And in Detroit the headlines caused a strange reaction: "What are the papers doing? Trying to keep the Tigers from winning the pennant?"

But Joe Sparma stood behind his remarks because he had said what he felt.

AUGUST 16

In one summer Denny McLain had become a legendary figure.

Much of this legend had been created by those mob scenes at his locker, with the repartee this way and that. The legend had been enhanced by the number of times McLain waited in the dugout or clubhouse, an apparent loser, then suddenly converted into a winner by his teammates.

McLain himself talked about what he did between the white lines, on the ball field, as being the most vital thing. There would have been no legend of Denny McLain this summer if he had not performed expertly there. His personality dominated the legend. But his performance made it important. And often his performance was overlooked because of his personality.

On the drive to 30, the twenty-fifth victory tonight was very typical of McLain, the pitcher.

In the sixth inning McLain had a 2–0 lead, given him by Al Kaline's first homer in three weeks. His opponent was Jim Lonborg, who last year had been the best pitcher in the league.

Now in the sixth, with none out, Lonborg unexpectedly bunted toward third base. The pitcher, his ski-damaged knee healed, beat the ball out. Mike Andrews followed by slicing a single. The Boston fans are among the world's noisiest, and 35,323 were crammed into Fenway Park.

The two base runners advanced when Bill Freehan attempted to pick Lonborg off second and fired the ball into center field.

McLain was confronted with a runner on third, another on second, the noise and the deadly portion of the Red Sox's batting order. Boston needed only a single to tie the game.

McLain struck out Dalton Jones, the Tiger-killer.

The next batter was Carl Yastrzemski. McLain got two strikes on Yaz. The next four pitches, all fastballs, were over the plate, and Yaz fouled all four off. The next pitch was another fastball, and Yaz swung at it hard and missed. Two outs.

Mayo Smith walked to the mound. Ken Harrelson was still a hot hitter, and first base was vacant.

"Let's walk him," advised Smith.

"I'd rather pitch to him," responded McLain, his baseball cap perched over his nose.

Smith went against his judgment and was permissive with McLain. The pitcher kicked high and pitched to Harrelson. A slider. Strike one. The second pitch, another slider, strike two.

McLain again kicked high and threw his third straight slider aimed for the outside corner. Harrelson swung and missed. Strike three, three outs. Lonborg and Andrews were stranded on base.

The Tigers won the ball game, 4–0, for their fourteenth victory in the past eighteen games. McLain was 25–3, five away from the thirty—and he had six shutouts and a 1.87 earned-run average. He was 16–0 on the road.

The lead jumped back to eight games over the beaten Orioles. Even Freehan wasn't especially upset because Lonborg had hit him three times with pitched balls.

Not even Mayo was upset. He conferred with Joe Sparma for 15 minutes and did not fine him.

AUGUST 17

"Too damn hot," muttered Bill Freehan. It was 90 degrees in Fenway Park this afternoon. Freehan swallowed a salt tablet and took a swig of orange juice.

Thankfully, it was an easy ball game, a laugher. In the sixth inning the Tigers had themselves an 8–1 advantage over the Red Sox.

But then in the bottom of the sixth the Red Sox scored and scored and scored until they had seven runs. They tied the game, 8–8, as the Tigers tried and couldn't get the outs.

When the inning finally ended, Freehan staggered to the clubhouse, changed to a fresh baseball suit and took another salt tablet.

Norm Cash singled in a run in the eighth to get the Tigers back in front, 9–8. But with one out in the bottom of the ninth, Ken Harrelson clubbed a home run over the chummy left-field wall to tie the game again, 9–9.

"I can barely hold the bat," said Freehan as he went to the plate in the eleventh.

There were two outs—and he hit the ball into the nets atop the left-field fence for a 10–9 lead.

The Red Sox attempted to retaliate once again in the bottom of the eleventh. With two outs, Carl Yastrzemski singled, and then Harrelson singled. Mayo Smith called in John Wyatt, who last summer had pitched for the Red Sox and then feuded with Dick Williams.

Wyatt got Rico Petrocelli on a fly to center, and the long hot afternoon was ended. They had played nearly four hours in the heat.

Last Licks Victory Number Twenty-two was one of the most difficult.

"I'm so tired that my ears are ringing and my eyes won't focus," said Freehan. "I must have lost twelve pounds."

The catcher had swallowed a dozen salt tablets, washed them down with orange juice and put on three uniform shirts and two pairs of pants.

"They should have had a reliever in there for me," said the abused Norm Cash.

He hit a home run and four other hits, driving in five runs. During the past three weeks, he had a .400 batting average.

"I worked that out myself," said Cash. "Is .400 any good?"

AUGUST 18

Three Red Sox bunts beat the Tigers, 4–1, this afternoon.

But the 14-game stretch against the Red Sox and Indians was over. The Tigers had taken the two contenders, 11 games to 3 in the dozen days.

They flew home, exhausted. Denny McLain went to New York.

AUGUST 19

Somebody asked Bob Gibson about the first game of the World Series and how he felt about pitching against Denny McLain.

"The hell with McLain," responded Gibson. "We haven't won the pennant yet, and Detroit isn't in yet either."

"That's right," said McLain when told of Gibson's remark. "I agree with him."

It was an off-day for the Tigers, a busy day for the virtuoso in New York.

"I was up at five thirty in the morning to go to the *Today Show*," said McLain. "I got back to the Essex House at a quarter of eight and had interviews until noon. There was *Time*, *Life*, UPI. At noon, I was at the Hampshire House and played a few numbers.

"At twelve twenty I went to lunch with my business manager, Frank Scott. At one thirty there were more interviews. At three o'clock, I went to the Hampshire House and got ready to do the show. The show was at four twenty until five. Then there were more interviews till seven fifteen.

"Then I went to a meeting with the Hammond Organ people till ten o'clock. I returned to the Essex House. Then I went to the airport.

"The midnight plane left at twelve fifty-five. It got to Detroit at two thirty. I got home at three fifteen and to bed at four."

McLain had been moving for twenty-two and a half hours. From one of the interviews in New York there came a wire story that he had been pitching with a torn shoulder muscle.

AUGUST 20

For nearly a month, since Joe Sparma on July 25, no start-ing pitcher except Denny McLain had pitched a complete game for the Tigers.

Tonight there was another of those twi-night doublehead-ers, with the White Sox.

John Hiller pitched a complete game. Only a single in the fifth inning by Ron Hansen prevented Hiller from pitching a no-hitter.

He beat the White Sox, 7–0.

Hiller revealed he had presented his wife with a dozen roses for her birthday but wouldn't let her attend the game.

"Superstition," said Hiller.

"Janice is superstitious?" asked a writer.

"No, I am," said the pitcher.

Once, when he had been a kid pitcher outside Toronto, his parents came to watch Hiller play. He was pounded. Ever since then he wanted his family away when he pitched.

Following Hiller's one-hitter, Denny McLain went out to pitch the second game in quest of victory number twenty-six.

Pete Ward hit a grand slam home run off him, and the Tigers committed four errors. Mayo Smith relieved McLain in the sixth inning when he was losing, 9–2, with seven of the runs unearned.

The Tigers lost, 10–2, and McLain was beaten for the fourth time.

Denny had had two more meetings during the day with his quartet—"I call it a quartet, it's really a quintet now"—and with Frank Scott.

"There are so many things I can do," he said. "I have to give it the personal touch.

"I really don't think it affects the pitching. I wouldn't let it affect the pitching."

His 25–4 record was convincing.

The torn shoulder muscle?

"It's nothing real, real serious," McLain said. "It's not exactly torn. It's torn to the extent that it's stretched.

"The other night in Boston I had the best stuff I'd had all year. Tonight I had the worst stuff all year. I couldn't even finesse them."

McLain had been taking treatments to relieve a strain in his shoulder.

The 49,000 people in the park had seen a rarity in the second game. Al Kaline, after a run, dropped a fly ball. It was, as far Tiger watchers could remember, the first time in the history of baseball that Kaline had dropped a fly ball. He also was charged with a throwing error.

"I've dropped them before," he insisted, but nobody could remember. Including the people. They booed and booed and booed Kaline. The Tigers had gone into command of the race when he was hurt in June, and the people reminded him of that. There were many times when Mayo Smith had him sitting on the bench, and they reminded him of that.

Al Kaline's team was in first place, but he was not a key factor after all these years.

Already, a problem was starting to concern Smith. If the Tigers got into the World Series, what would he do with Kaline?

The outfield had been Horton, Stanley and Northrup when the Tigers were on their June surge. Kaline had been utility man, almost, since he'd come back in July.

How could Mayo break up the outfield that helped the Tigers to their large lead?

How could the Tigers play in the World Series, after twenty-three years, without Al Kaline on the field?

There was going to be a dilemma for Mayo Smith, if the Tigers didn't fold.

"This has been a rewarding season," Kaline said. "It's been

fun. The boos? They're disappointed more than anything. They always expect me to be good."

But inside, Kaline burned and hurt.

Sixteen years here and the club finally was directed toward a pennant and the people were booing him.

AUGUST 21

Before tonight's game, as the umpires took their positions, Emmett Ashford took a flying leap over the pitcher's mound en route to second base. The crowd applauded.

Then the Tigers ran to their positions and Norm Cash took a broad jump over the pitcher's mound on the way to first base.

Ashford doffed his cap to Cash.

Until the eighth inning the people had nothing else to amuse them. The White Sox led, 2–1. Bob Locker, a relief pitcher, was handling the Tigers with ease.

For 18 games through 30 innings, Locker had not permitted a run.

With two outs in the eighth, Mickey Stanley tied the score with a home run. In the tenth, Mayo Smith sent Jim Price up to pinch-hit for reliever Daryl Patterson.

"Why don't you get a haircut, kid?" yelled a customer, perhaps a barber, to Price.

"Imagine a guy worried about a haircut at a time like that," said Price.

Price took his cut and drove the ball into the lower left-field seats for the 3–2 victory. There was the usual reception group at home plate.

"I'm still shaking," said Price in the clubhouse. "I'm more nervous after I pinch-hit than when I go up there."

He took a swig of the soft drink Denny McLain used to endorse.

"How'd you like to win thirty games?" said a writer.

"I'd just like to catch Denny in thirty games," said Price.

It was Last Licks Victory Number Twenty-three.

AUGUST 22

The Tigers had their own favorite ballplayer. If they had the franchise to vote for the Most Valuable Player, instead of the writers, their selection would be Dick McAuliffe. Mac is a tough Irish-Italian kid from Connecticut, and he came out of the farm system in the early sixties as a shortstop.

He had flaws as a fielder and a peculiar batting style. He cocked his bat high and then kicked his front leg toward the pitch.

Mac hit pretty well that way, and he was a reliable clutch hitter. Mac's batting into the double play that ended last year's pennant race haunted him.

It was his fight, his spirit, that appealed to his teammates. Twice Mac made the All-Star team as the starting shortstop. Then Mayo Smith came to Detroit to manage last year. Mayo's first maneuver was to convert McAuliffe into a second baseman. Mac was shaky at the spot, and double-play footwork troubled him. But this season he developed into a polished second baseman. And his aggressiveness helped the Tigers win.

One week earlier in the summer Mac hit four routine singles and his daring baserunning turned all four into doubles.

"He can play second base now, and he's another reason why we're in first place," said Smith.

Tonight Mickey Lolich was liberated from his bullpen exile after winning four games in relief. Smith started him against the White Sox and Tommy John.

McAuliffe led off in the first with a single and went around to score the first run. In the third, he batted again.

John's second pitch was tucked under Mac's chin. Mc-Auliffe turned around and said something to umpire Al Salerno.

"If he hits me in the head, I'm dead," said Mac.

Another pitch sailed in close. Mac glared at the pitcher. John's three and two pitch for ball four again was tucked under Mac's chin. Mac sprawled into the dirt face down. He arose, dropped his bat and started toward first base. He started jawing at John. John started talking back.

About 30 feet down the line, Mac took a 90-degree left turn and rushed at John. John stepped in and then braced, ready to throw a shoulder block on the charger. He did with his left shoulder, an integral section of his pitching mechanism. McAuliffe went over John. They tumbled to the ground together, Mac on top.

Players ran from the two dugouts, and the fight was quickly broken up. John walked away from the milling ballplayers clutching his left shoulder. Salerno raised his thumb, ejecting McAuliffe, and apparently John was banished, too.

"I wasn't going to be a guinea pig," said McAuliffe. "I wasn't going to stand there and let him hit me in the head with his fastball."

John had torn ligaments in his shoulder and wouldn't be able to pitch again for at least three weeks.

"Why would I throw at him on a three-two pitch?" asked John.

Salerno said he would state in his report to Joe Cronin, the league president, that Mac was the aggressor.

"I doubt he'll be suspended, though," said Salerno. "I don't think John was throwing at him on a three-two pitch. But John did cuss him."

Salerno said both combatants were ejected.

The game proceeded with Denny Ribant, the discarded Tiger, pitching for the Sox. By the sixth, Ribant had a 2–1 lead.

Then Al Kaline hit his eighth homer deep to left center

It all began with a close pitch by Chicago's Tommy John which sent Dick McAuliffe into the dirt (1). On the way to first, McAuliffe and John go at each other (2) and the Tiger lands on top (3). John walks off the field with torn ligaments in his arm (4).

and Willie Horton followed with his twenty-ninth. Lolich scored another run when he beat out a single and came around to score with a bouncing slide.

Smith took Lolich out of the game right there—knocked out by his own base hit and baserunning. Don McMahon pitched two relief innings to make Lolich a 4–2 winner.

Lolich spoke after the game about his release from the fenced-in bullpen.

"You're the loneliest man on the field there," he said.

Smith's timing for removal of his starting pitcher was unusual. He had let him bat and then run, shunning use of a pinch hitter or runner.

"He ran out of gas," Smith explained. "He didn't even have a tiger in his tank."

Around the corner at his locker, Denny McLain said he missed the fight. He wasn't among the Tigers who'd run onto the field.

"Do you know where I was during the fight?" he said with his pixie grin. "I was here in the training room eating a hot dog."

At the pressroom bar Mayo Smith discussed baseball. He was talking about the way Ribant had handled the Tigers for almost three innings before the two homers.

"I don't get mad often," said Mayo, "but I started walking up and down the dugout telling them, 'If you let this ———— beat you, you better give up.' Just then, Kaline boom, Horton boom."

Smith informed the writers he was going to pitch Joe Sparma in New York tomorrow night. It would be Sparma's first appearance since he had been taken out in Cleveland and denounced the move.

"You want to come to New York and watch Sparma struggle, struggle, struggle?" said Smith. "I'll tell you this, he better pitch well or he'll be out of there early."

AUGUST 23

This morning Ed Short, the bland, humorless general manager of the White Sox, called Joe Cronin on the telephone. Short called to discuss the incident between Dick McAuliffe and Tommy John and umpire Al Salerno's telegrammed report.

"I told him it was our position that McAuliffe should be suspended for making such an unprovoked attack," Short told a Chicago newspaperman. "I told him that we had to have protection for our players."

Cronin said Salerno's report mentioned that McAuliffe had been ejected but not John.

A telegram already was en route to McAuliffe in New York telling him the league had fined him $250.

After talking with Short, Cronin had a second telegram dispatched to McAuliffe. This one informed him that in addition to the fine he was suspended for five days.

Cronin had an assistant telephone Mayo Smith. At Yankee Stadium, Mac learned of his suspension from reporters.

"I want a chance to tell my side," said McAuliffe, crestfallen.

Jim Campbell, the Tigers' general manager, now tracked down Cronin in Minneapolis. Cronin told Campbell the Tigers had no recourse. The suspension was firm. McAuliffe could not play in the series with the Yankees and the following series with the White Sox.

The Tigers felt Short had pressured Cronin into the five-day suspension. They were irate at the loss of their spark plug during an important part of the pennant race. Ed Short was upset because the Tigers weren't punished more severely.

"Boy, that's sure equitable," Short said in Chicago. "We lose a man for twenty-one days and they lose a man for five days. I don't think McAuliffe's punishment was sufficient."

"Cronin used bad judgment," said Campbell. "The injury to John shouldn't have entered into this thing. It was too bad it happened, but he tried to tackle Mac."

Hal Middlesworth, the Tigers' publicity man, said there had been a check with Salerno immediately after the fight to ask if John also had been heaved from the game.

"He told us John had been ejected, too," Middlesworth said. "We announced that in the press box."

"I haven't seen a pitcher yet get five days for hitting anyone on the head," said Bill Freehan, the authority on being hit by a baseball.

Smith could hardly control his anger.

"John hit us four times in Chicago in June," said Smith. "They hit eight of our guys in the series there and we didn't hit any of theirs.

"I've seen a lot of batters thrown at in a three-two situation. And I think both sides should be given a hearing in a matter such as this."

Hearing? Cronin had made himself inaccessible, vanished some place in Minnesota. His office in Boston said he'd be back next week.

The Tigers went out to play the Yankees in a twi-nighter without Mac, their spirit leader.

They lost the first game, 2–1. Their only run was Earl Wilson's home run. Then in the sixth Wilson was hit again by a line drive back to the mound, a smash by Joe Pepitone. For the fourth time this year, Wilson was out of a game due to injury.

There was an acute infielder shortage with McAuliffe suspended and Tom Matchick back home for Guard duty. Mayo was curtailed as a maneuverer. Finally in the late innings he needed a shortstop. He brought Mickey Stanley in from center field and made him a shortstop, the Tigers' fifth of the year.

Joe Sparma reappeared as the starting pitcher in the second game. Stanley started the game at shortstop. Sparma had a 2–1 lead in the sixth inning, and when the Yankees threatened, Smith took him out. In the eighth the Tigers scored again, but the Yankees scored twice on Roy White's homer.

It was 3–3, and the game went into extra innings. The Yankees and Tigers played through 11 innings of scorelessness. After 19 innings, or five hours and four minutes of baseball, the second game was terminated at 1:07 A.M. by the curfew. It would have to be replayed as a brand new game Sunday, part of a doubleheader.

It had been a bitter day and night for the Tigers, a shocking day. But still they did not lose any of their seven-and-a-half-game lead over Baltimore.

At least Denny McLain would be pitching the next game against the Yankees.

On the bus downtown, Stanley spoke of his emergency role as a shortstop.

"There's too much tension there and it wears you out," he said.

AUGUST 24

Even Denny McLain on the road couldn't revive the Tigers this afternoon. For the first time he lost two in a row. He was hung up on a number, 26, and now had five losses. For the first time, he lost on the road. He had been 16–0 on the road before Roy White hit a two-run homer to beat him today.

"I never should have thrown that pitch," said Denny. "I never should have let White have a fastball like that."

It was the only bad pitch McLain made, but it beat him. Mel Stottlemyre made one bad pitch, too, and Willie Horton hit his thirtieth home run. But White had a runner on base ahead of him, and the Yankees won, 2–1.

Dick McAuliffe watched from a box seat as Mayo Smith maneuvered. Tom Matchick flew in after his Army duty and played second base. Later he went to shortstop. Mayo again brought Mickey Stanley into the infield. This time he became the Tigers' fifth second baseman of the year.

In the clubhouse the Tigers sat in front of their lockers, fatigued from 37 innings of nonwinning baseball in 23 hours. They seemed beaten, demoralized, with another doubleheader confronting them tomorrow.

AUGUST 25

"Don't knock the Rock, but don't let him pitch."

The late Eddie Jones had written that in the Toledo *Blade* ten years ago when Rocky Colavito, on a lark, had done some pitching. Now a decade later the Yankees' pitching staff was hard up due to doubleheader overwork. The Rock came out of the outfield today for the second time to pitch.

The Yankees were losing the first game to the Tigers, 5–1, and Ralph Houk decided not to expend one of his pitchers. So he had Colavito warm up and come in to pitch. Colavito worked out of a jam by getting Al Kaline and Willie Horton. Then he pitched two more innings and Kaline got the only hit.

In the bottom of the sixth inning Pat Dobson was coasting with the four-run lead and two outs. Andy Kosco hit a routine fly ball into the left field no-man's-land at Yankee Stadium. Horton drifted back.

"I had it all the way," said Horton. "But just before I could catch it the ball went into the haze. It was then I lost it."

"Turn your head," yelled Mickey Stanley, who had come over from center field.

Horton did, and Kosco's fly ball hit him on the shoulder. The ball fell to the grass for a double. The Yankees proceeded to score five runs with two outs.

Colavito was the winning pitcher, 6–5.

Mickey Lolich started the second game for Detroit. He couldn't locate home plate and walked seven Yankees in the first three innings. Colavito, back in right field, touched him for a home run. The Tigers lost, 5–4.

They had lost four straight games, their longest losing streak, since Dick McAuliffe was suspended. Each of the four losses was by one run.

Worsening the depression was a new injury to Al Kaline, a pulled thigh muscle.

"I thought I'd get my anger over in a couple of days," said Jim Campbell. "But I got madder. It's the most unfair decision I've seen in baseball. I'm not as disturbed at the fine and the suspension as I am at Cronin's attitude."

The Tigers felt McAuliffe had been deprived of a hearing.

"I'm not accusing Cronin of trying to even up the pennant race by having us lose a few games. I've never said that and I don't think it. But look what losing McAuliffe is doing to us. He's probably the most valuable player on our team, in the whole league for that matter."

And down in Baltimore the Orioles struggled for 18 innings and beat the Red Sox, 3–2. They suddenly were only five games back with a three-game visit to Detroit next weekend.

The Tigers had been edgy, watching the scoreboard, hoping the Red Sox could win. There was tension when they sat exhausted at their lockers after 55 innings of futility in Yankee Stadium.

Bill Freehan walked over to the blackboard in the visitors' clubhouse beneath the stands. He picked up a piece of chalk and printed a message to his teammates:

> ANYBODY WHO THINKS THE WORLD ENDED TODAY
> DOESN'T BELONG HERE.

AUGUST 26

"If we lose it, it'll be my fault, you know," Earl Wilson had told Pete Waldmeir, the columnist of the Detroit *News*.

That remark was recalled as Wilson, his body bruised, started to pitch tonight in the Tigers' one-game visit to Milwaukee. The opposition was the White Sox, and they dearly wanted to tighten the pressure around the necks of the Tigers.

Wilson beat them, 3–0, with a six-hitter. He drove in two of the runs himself.

It was Eddie Mathews Night. The good burghers of Milwaukee cheered and cheered the man who had been their hero when the Braves played and won pennants there. Jim Campbell announced that Mathews, recovered from his serious operation, would be restored to the active roster on September 1 when the player limit was raised.

And still Joe Cronin was unavailable, reported en route back to Boston. In Detroit a pursuing reporter tried half the night to locate Cronin for his still unexplained version of Dick McAuliffe's suspension.

AUGUST 27

An early morning call to the American League headquarters in Boston was answered with the secretarial statement that Joe Cronin was tied up on the phone. "He'll call you back."

Ninety minutes and two more Detroit-to-Boston calls later the communication gap was broken. Cronin was lured to the telephone.

"Oh, I didn't know anyone was trying to reach me," said the American League president.

Reporter: "Why did you suspend McAuliffe?"

Cronin: "There's a rule in the book that calls for a penalty for an unwarranted attack on the ball field, and it's up to the league president's discretion. He was suspended on the basis of being the aggressor and his attack on the pitcher. You can't stand for that in baseball. You have a pretty good pitcher. Suppose a utility player went out rapping a bat at McLain's head?"

Reporter: "But McAuliffe dropped his bat at home plate?"

Cronin: "It comes automatically for a fight. The rule book says thirty days. This time I said five. I thought thirty was too severe in the heat of the pennant race."

Reporter: "There's confusion about whether Al Salerno ejected both McAuliffe and John. Did Salerno's report say that both players had been ejected?"

Cronin: "I'm reading you the wire from umpire Al Salerno: 'Joseph Cronin—Ejected Dick McAuliffe third inning tonight for attack on pitcher Tommy John.' "

Reporter: "Did the injury to John have any bearing on the suspension?"

Cronin: "I didn't know about the injury until after I made my decision."

Reporter: "How come there have been other fights in which the players were not suspended, such as the one the Tigers were involved in at Oakland in May?"

Cronin: "They all vary. I think it is the heat of the pennant race. There is no doubt in my mind that McAuliffe was the aggressor. Is this inquisition over?"

The Tigers traveled on to Chicago for tonight's game with the White Sox. But Denny McLain had flown to Detroit for X ray treatment for his tired, sore shoulder.

This was the last game of McAuliffe's suspension. Tom Matchick was the second baseman.

The score was 1–1 entering the ninth. Matchick led off with a single, and the Tigers loaded the bases with none out. But Willie Horton bounded back to pitcher Wilbur Wood, who started a double play via home plate. The Tigers still had men on second and third. Norm Cash, whose twentieth homer had accounted for the Tigers' run, slapped the ball toward left field.

Luis Aparicio, the shortstop, was stationed toward second

base for Cash. Aparicio charged to his right, scooped up Cash's ball and nipped him at first base with a strong throw. The Tigers failed to score, and it was still 1–1 in the bottom of the ninth.

Buddy Bradford reached second with one out. Aparicio then hit a ball through the pitcher's box and Matchick skidded to his right to take it. Aparicio was flying down the line and Matchick hurried his throw. The ball skipped into the dirt and over Cash's glove. On the errant throw, Bradford scored the winning run.

It was a last licks loss, 2–1, and the Tigers were now in danger. The Orioles won a doubleheader. The lead was cut to four games, the shortest it had been since June.

The suspension was over and the Tigers had lost five of their six decisions while McAuliffe was out. Every one of the five defeats was by one run.

"The suspension had to have an effect," said Mayo Smith, still angry. "Mac'd have won some of them. He'd have gotten a hit here or there, like in that nineteen-inning game."

The Tigers went home for series with the Angels and then three games with the Orioles.

AUGUST 28

Bill Rigney, the Angels' jittery and witty manager, thought the situation was humorous.

"We were the ones who knocked out Detroit last year," he said. "Wouldn't it be funny if we did it again? We have five games left with them."

The old reputation for folding up under pressure was being recalled again.

ORIOLES KEEP GAINING AS TIGERS CRACK, blurted the headline in one Baltimore newspaper.

FLAG FEVER SPREADS, said another Baltimore paper.

The Orioles figured to go to Detroit with momentum. While the Tigers were playing the Angels twice, the Orioles had two games with Washington. They had beaten the Senators twelve of twelve.

Denny McLain pitched for the sinking Tigers tonight. Bill Freehan was the first baseman as Mayo Smith did some more maneuvering.

And Dick McAuliffe was back as second baseman. On his first trip to the plate, the Angels' pitcher, Tom Burgmeier, fired a pitch close to Mac's head. McAuliffe got up and stepped back up to the plate, rather perturbed.

In the second, Freehan hit a two-run homer as the Tigers scored three times.

In the eighth, Freehan was hit by a pitch for the twenty-second time. He rolled in the dirt, tapped home plate with his fingers, got up and spoke to umpire Ed Runge.

"I talked to the umpire about Mr. Cronin's decision," said Freehan. Then he took that football player's jog to first base.

Jim Northrup cracked a home run and Freehan came around, glaring at pitcher Bobby Locke all the way. The Tigers won, 6–1.

McLain broke his two-game losing streak with his twenty-sixth victory, finally. This made him the first to win that many in the American League in twenty-two years.

"How can you throw like that with your shoulder so sore?" asked a writer.

"Because we were only four games ahead of Baltimore," said McLain.

For the twelfth time in his 26 victories, McLain was the Tigers' stopper—winning after a loss.

At Baltimore, Frank Howard lofted a 420-foot home run and the Senators defeated the Orioles for the first time, 3–2.

The lead was reopened to five games.

AUGUST 29

Earlier this month, while imprisoned in the fenced-in bull-pen dugout, Mickey Lolich had thought about the World Series. There is time to think out there. Lolich wondered what Mayo Smith's plans for him would be if the Tigers won the pennant.

"Before I'd gone out there, I figured I would pitch the third game here in Detroit," said Lolich. "I thought Denny would pitch the first game and Earl the second in St. Louis and then I thought we'd use a left-hander in our park here because of the short right field.

"I kept thinking about that even when I was in the bull-pen."

The released Lolich had difficulties in the first two innings of this afternoon's start against the Angels. He gave up three hits. In the first, Smith signaled to the bullpen for a pitcher to warm up, and out of the enclosure stepped Joe Sparma. Even Smith recognized the hideous humor of the situation. Lolich caught the thought out on the mound—he was in trouble.

"I thought all I have to do now is pop off and everything would be complete," he said.

After allowing the three hits in the first two innings, Lolich permitted the Angels no more. He retired 20 straight batters.

Willie Horton hit his thirty-first home run into the right-field seats—where he hit that one years ago in the high school championship game.

The Tigers won, 2–0, and it was Lolich's sixth victory of the month, his second since taken out of the bullpen.

He then zoomed home in the rush-hour traffic on his red motorcycle.

Malcolm W. Emmons

Mickey Lolich

Tonight the Orioles and Senators scrambled into extra innings. Then the Senators scored in the eleventh and won, 5–4.

The Orioles boarded their airplane for Detroit and the three-game series, six games behind.

Bill Rigney had a parting comment, too, for his old buddy, Mayo.

"If the Tigers win one of the three with Baltimore, or two," said Rig, "it will just about be over."

AUGUST 30

GO GET 'EM, TIGERS!!! exhorted the bulb light sign on the Lodge Expressway near the ball park exit. There was a massive traffic jam as 53,575 people were on their way to the first game of the series with the Orioles.

Mayo Smith entrusted Earl Wilson with the start. Wilson faced Tom Phoebus, the stocky right-hander who had won 13 games for the Orioles.

In the second inning Phoebus hit Bill Freehan on the shoulder. It was the twenty-third time Freehan had been hit, putting his name in the record book. Tommy Matchick then hit a single.

Up came Wilson and he took a mighty cut. The ball streaked into the left-field seats for his fifth homer.

On the expressway, in the still-poking traffic jam, listeners to Ernie Harwell's broadcast leaned on their car horns in a raucous, exuberant symphony. In the ball park the largest crowd in seven years deafened one another with the noise. The Tigers led, 3–0.

The next inning Jim Northrup doubled, Norm Cash doubled, Freehan doubled, Don Wert singled, and Wilson singled. The Tigers scored five more runs.

"I'll be there when they need me," Wilson had said at a time when he had been blaming himself.

He won on a four-hitter, 9–1, tonight for his second very much needed victory of the week. Wilson had given up one run as a pitcher and driven in six as a hitter in the two games.

"If we win tomorrow and Sunday we'll be right back in it," said Earl Weaver, the Orioles' manager. "I didn't make much of a speech after the game—all I said was, 'Fellas, now we've got to win them all.'

"I figured before this series we had to win five of the six games we had left with Detroit here this weekend and next month. Now we've lost one and have five left."

In the Tigers' clubhouse Mayo Smith was seated at his desk, trying to be calm. An agitator asked him to admit that the Tigers had the pennant won now. Mayo's hawk face contorted and turned red.

"Leo Durocher said it one year with the Giants," said the reporter.

"Where did he finish?" asked Mayo.

"Second," came the reply.

Now the Orioles had a three-game losing streak and the Tigers had won three straight. The lead was seven games again.

AUGUST 31

"Say, how'd Baltimore come out today?" yelled Norm Cash in that Texas ranch slur of his, and it broke the brooding in the clubhouse.

It had been a question the Tigers had asked the scoreboard watchers regularly in the past weeks with the pennant race tightened.

Baltimore won today, Detroit lost. The Orioles took the second game of the series with the Tigers, 5–1.

Dave McNally beat the Tigers with Paul Blair's help. Blair hit a triple for the first run and then a three-run homer off John Hiller.

"If we beat them tomorrow, the pressure's back on them," said Earl Weaver.

"If we win tomorrow, we'll put more pressure on them," retaliated Mayo Smith from the comfort of first place. "It's tougher to play catch up. Tomorrow's an important game—there's a big difference between five ahead and seven ahead."

The Tigers were headed into the September stretch still remembering last year—but this time they were ahead, by six games. And they had Denny McLain going for them again tomorrow.

SEPTEMBER 1

As was discovered long ago, Denny McLain had this flair for showmanship, this knack of doing things a little differently. What other ballplayer had met his future wife when his bat flew into the grandstands at a kids' game and struck her? Who else in the big leagues played the organ?

Rain this Sunday afternoon held the crowd down to 41,698. It was evident at the beginning that McLain did not have his best stuff.

Don Buford led off the game with a single. Then Curt Blefary pounded the ball into the right-field stands. Before McLain had a man out, he was behind, 2–0. In the bottom of the first, Jim Northrup tied it up for him.

Then, in the second, the Tigers scored twice more. By the

third, the rain had held the game up twice for a total of 74 minutes. The field was sloppy.

The Orioles got to McLain again in the third. Buford walked and Blefary and Frank Robinson singled to cut the Tigers' lead to 4–3.

Mayo Smith had Pat Dobson warming up. McLain was struggling, and if Boog Powell got a hit, Mayo was going to relieve with Dobson.

Powell is one of the giants of baseball, one of the strongest men. He connected squarely with McLain's pitch. The ball was lined with terrifying speed right back to the box.

McLain stuck up his glove for protection and the ball stuck squarely in the pocket. He whirled and threw to shortstop Tom Matchick at second base. Blefary was out. Matchick relayed the ball to Norm Cash at first and it beat Robinson back. He, too, was out.

A triple play. How else would Denny McLain escape danger?

McLain carried on to win his twenty-seventh game, 7–2. For the thirteenth time he was the stopper.

"I never saw the ball," he told the enlarged audience.

"Where did you catch it?" asked a reporter.

"Here," said McLain. He tapped his forehead. "I think if I still had my glasses on, it had me. It's instinct."

"What kind of pitch did Blefary hit?"

"A bad pitch," said McLain.

"What kind of pitch did Powell hit?"

"A good pitch," said McLain.

"What did you and Powell talk about when you got to first base in the bottom of the inning after the triple play?"

"He said, 'I'm snake-bit,'" said McLain. "I got to agree with him.

"The first couple of innings are always tough, especially since I've come up with the bad arm. The triple play woke me up.

"I saw the ball off the bat. But not all the way."

"What about the race now?"

"I think the pennant race is getting near over," said McLain.

The same answer was sought from Mayo Smith. Mayo rocked in his swivel chair.

"Wellllllllll," he said finally. "This is my thirty-sixth year in baseball. Everybody's trying to get me to say it. But there's time left and we could get a lot of injuries."

"What about McLain's organ playing?"

"I'm a music lover, but I'm not a musician," said Mayo Smith.

Yes, he agreed, he'd prefer to have his star pitcher an organ player like McLain than a skier like Jim Lonborg, who wrecked his knee on the ski slopes.

The Tigers had won their two of three from the Orioles and opened their lead to seven games. It was time for the magic number business, that mathematical projection that becomes popular near the end of every pennant race.

Detroit's magic number had dwindled to nineteen. Any combination of nineteen—victories by the Tigers or losses by the Orioles—and Detroit would have its first pennant in twenty-three years.

SEPTEMBER 4

On the long plane ride to Oakland the word could be used freely now—*pennant*. The Tigers used it in conversation that punctuated their card games and even the words *World Series* were no longer an unmentionable. Indeed Charley Creeden, the traveling secretary, won Jim Campbell's approval to tell the airline, yes, the Tigers would want to charter an airplane to St. Louis on September 30.

Bill Freehan and baseball writer George Cantor, two Detroit-born young men, had a conversation above the Rockies.

"Anyone who grew up in Detroit and followed sports knows how much this city wants a winner for the Tigers," said Freehan. "I think the pennant may mean even more to guys like myself, Willie Horton, Jim Northrup and Mickey Stanley, who were raised in Michigan, than to the other players."

Jim Nash shut out the Tigers, 4–0, in the opener of the Labor Day doubleheader. In the first inning of the second game Stanley made another magnificent catch in center field. He ran and ran and caught Reggie Jackson's drive an instant before plowing into the center-field fence. Stanley returned the ball to the infield and then collapsed to the grass. When he regained his wind, he stayed in the ball game.

Joe Sparma started again and pitched six innings and had a 3–2 lead. The A's tied it with a run in the eighth. The game went into extra innings.

In the tenth, Freehan faced Diego Segui, who had not yielded a run for a month. Freehan socked the ball over the left-field wall and the Tigers won, 4–3.

It was Last Licks Victory Number Twenty-four. Pat Dobson was the winning pitcher with two innings of winless relief ball.

Earl Wilson started last night and hit another home run, his sixth. He had a 2–0 lead in the eighth. But the A's scored three times. The run that sent the A's ahead scored when Northrup booted a ball in right field.

In the top of the ninth, Ed Mathews, returned to the roster, walked. Dick McAuliffe singled and Stanley walked to load the bases. Bob Kennedy, the A's manager, brought in left-hander Warren Bogle to pitch to Northrup.

"You don't always get a second chance," Northrup said.

Northrup singled to right to drive in two runs and return the lead to the Tigers. They scored twice more and won,

6–3. Dobson again was the winning pitcher with one inning of hitless relief ball.

It was Last Licks Victory Number Twenty-five.

Tonight the score was tied, 2-all, in the Tigers' eighth, and there were two outs. Stanley walked and Northrup singled. Al Kaline, coming up on his sore leg, walked, and the bases again were filled. Kennedy summoned Jack Aker to face Horton.

Willie rapped the ball off Aker's glove and the winning run scored.

The 4–2 victory was the thirty-fifth the Tigers had earned with a rally after being either behind or tied as late as the seventh. This time John Hiller was the winner as the starter. But Pat Dobson again was needed and pitched one-hit relief ball over the last two innings.

The Tigers won three of four in Oakland and headed back home with the magic number reduced to fourteen. Their home-bred players—Freehan, Northrup, Horton and Stanley—were responsible for advancing the Tigers closer to the pennant.

Northrup, again the right-fielder with Kaline hurting the past two weeks, was on another hitting surge. He had got 21 hits in 47 at-bats since Kaline was hurt and had added 20 percentage points to his batting average.

This was the final visit to Oakland, and again Mayo Smith took precautions to keep the clubhouse sealed to all but writers. A guard was ordered to screen credentials. The security was necessary because of the suit filed when the ball was thrown into the stands and hit a woman last May.

At the visitors' clubhouse door a man presented his press card and was allowed admittance. He stood among the other press card bearers and asked Mayo a question or two. He jotted down the answers.

Suddenly the man stuck a piece of paper in Smith's hands.

The process server then fled the clubhouse.

SEPTEMBER 6

John Sain had been quiet and efficient through the season. He was Mayo Smith's pitching coach. The better bullpen, Mickey Lolich's comeback, Denny McLain's season . . . all were Sain's projects. Pat Dobson, John Hiller, Daryl Patterson and Fred Lasher had become big leaguers because of the work Sain did with them at spring training and before the ball games.

The Tigers' pitching staff was allowing a half-run less as a group than it did last year. Yet Sain was barely noticed— except by the pitchers he trained.

"My claim to fame is taking credit for something somebody else does," he said with characteristic modesty.

Denny McLain was very close now to becoming baseball's first 30-game winner in thirty-four years.

"The only one I saw with more pressure on him was Roger Maris in the year he hit sixty-one home runs," said Sain, who had been pitching with the Yankees that year of 1961.

McLain was tonight's pitcher at Tiger Stadium, and he walked through the dugout on his way to warmup. He stopped to look at the Twins' batting order taped on the wall of the dugout. The Twins had a new name, a rookie just brought up for a late- season look-see, Graig Nettles.

"Who's Nettles?" asked McLain. "Is he a low ball or high ball hitter?"

"Low ball," said Mayo Smith.

In the first inning Dick McAuliffe, Mickey Stanley and Al Kaline, tonight the first baseman, hit successive singles off Jim Kaat. The Tigers had no outs and a run in.

Willie Horton came up, and the cheers of the 42,269 deafened him. Horton cracked his thirty-second home run into the left-field grandstand.

McLain had a 4–0 lead in the first.

In the Twins' dugout, manager Cal Ermer grabbed the telephone and dialed a number.

The bell rang on the red telephone at PR man Hal Middlesworth's seat in the press box on the third deck.

"Get Boswell up," said Ermer.

"What?" said the voice.

"Get Boswell up," repeated Ermer.

"This is the press box," said the voice. "Who's this?"

"This is the Minnesota dugout," said the caller. "What's the number of the bullpen?"

A moment or two later, Dave Boswell emerged from the bullpen dugout in the right-field corner and started to warm up.

In the second, McLain pitched to Nettles for the first time. The rookie whacked the ball into the right-field seats for his first big league homer.

"What? You think that's something new?" said McLain. "I hope that wasn't his first major league at-bat."

McLain was assured that Nettles had played a couple of games before coming to Detroit.

"Good, I've never done that," said McLain.

The Tigers won, 8–3, and McLain had his twenty-eighth victory—two away from his personal magic number. Horton drove in five of the runs. Denny struck out twelve Twins and was approaching Hal Newhouser's club strikeout record.

"I don't care about it," said McLain. "I've got another goal now."

He reflected on the value of 30 victories.

"Do you think Mr. Campbell knows what I want yet?" wondered McLain.

The Tigers, with a four-game winning streak, had opened their lead to nine games over the Orioles. The magic number was twelve.

SEPTEMBER 8

The Tigers learned that maybe Graig Nettles was indeed a low ball hitter. And a high ball hitter, too.

By this afternoon, the Tigers were brushing him back at the plate.

Yesterday he hit two homers off Pat Dobson, 2–1. The second was in the ninth, making it a last licks loss.

Today, he hit another one—with two runners on—to drive in all the Twins runs as they defeated the Tigers, 3–1.

The Tigers now had to travel west again, to California.

"Who's pitching for the Angels?" asked Al Kaline.

"Two left-handers in the series," Kaline was informed.

"Hey, I'll get to play two days," Al said.

The problem was intensifying for Mayo Smith—how could he get his four outfielders into the World Series and keep Norm Cash in the lineup against the Cardinals' right-handed pitching staff?

"I win Tuesday at Anaheim and then I have two and a half weeks to do it," said Denny McLain as he left the clubhouse.

SEPTEMBER 9

Denny McLain spent the day doing the Hollywood bit. He conferred with TV's Smothers Brothers and their staff.

"We were at Tommy Smothers' home," said McLain. "What a pad! It's worth three fifty to four hundred thousand dollars. I want one like it some day."

McLain got to Anaheim Stadium in time to do his regular 10 minutes of throwing, his routine for the day before he pitches.

Mickey Lolich won tonight's ball game, 6–0, with a two-hitter against the Angels. Willie Horton, Al Kaline and Mickey Stanley hit homers. It was the fourteenth victory for Lolich.

SEPTEMBER 10

Ed Sullivan, the stolid TV personality, was looking for the Tigers' clubhouse. Ray Lane, one of the Tigers' broadcasters, found him and led him to Denny McLain. Denny took Sullivan around the room and introduced him to the Tigers.

TV personality Ed Sullivan gets the pitch from Denny McLain.

UPI

McLain would be pitching for number twenty-nine tonight—and already was committed to Sullivan's Sunday night show after the World Series.

Denny leafed through the new issue of *Life* angrily. There were pages of pictures showing him yawning, reclining and goofing around in the Tigers' dugout, illustrating an uncomplimentary story.

Peeved, yet exhilarated, McLain went out to seek number twenty-nine.

He had a 1–0 lead over the Angels when he came to bat for the first time in the third inning. McLain bashed the ball off the center-field wall 400 feet away and made a jaunty slide into third for a triple. Dick McAuliffe drove him home with a single for the second run.

Later McLain hit two singles himself and drove in two more runs. He won number twenty-nine by a 7–2 score and struck out twelve Angels.

"I wish I were going after number thirty tomorrow," McLain said. He'd have to wait till Saturday.

After the ball game, McLain introduced Glen Campbell, the new pop ballad singer, around the clubhouse. They left together.

"I always wanted to be in show business," McLain told Campbell.

SEPTEMBER 11

Bill Rigney, the soothsayer of the American League, had one final prediction for the Tigers.

"Detroit will beat the St. Louis club in the World Series," said the manager of the Angels.

The Tigers had just polished off his club for the third

straight night, 8–2. John Hiller pitched, the sixth straight starting pitcher to last the distance.

Willie Horton knocked two home runs to boost his total to thirty-five.

"Willie's swinging the bat better than he has all season," said Mayo Smith.

The Tigers flew back to Detroit and the climactic weekend of Denny McLain's shot at 30 with the magic number reduced to eight.

SEPTEMBER 13

Mickey Lolich was prepared for Denny McLain's thirtieth.

On the pillar in the middle of the home team clubhouse at Tiger Stadium the necessary directions had been posted by Lolich. They could be seen quickly by anyone rushing through the door.

ATTENTION SPORTSWRITERS
DENNY MC LAIN'S LOCKER THIS WAY————→

The tumult was at McLain's locker. Dizzy Dean, the last pitcher to win 30 back in 1934, had come up from Wiggins, Mississippi.

"I wanna be the first to congratulate him," said Dizzy.

Sandy Koufax got Denny on tape for tomorrow's pregame show. Sportswriters had flown in from around the nation and were clustered at McLain's locker.

Mickey Lolich sat on the stool, his potbelly rolled over the belt of his baseball knickers, at his own locker in another corner. He was alone except for one writer.

"How could I be a thirty-game winner?" said Lolich.

"How could I ride a motorcycle on the *Ed Sullivan Show?*

"I'm learning to play the drums, though. If I have a good year next year and win twenty, they'll say, 'So what?' He's sort of ruined things for everybody around here."

In his office Mayo Smith had the questioners ask him what kind of year he had anticipated for McLain at spring training. After all, McLain had been a figure in trade talks after his noncontribution in the failure of last September.

"On the performance of last year, yes, I'd have to say he was our fourth starter," Mayo said. "After he started pitching exhibition games, I saw he was better. I thought he could win twenty games."

"I thought I'd win twenty, twenty-five," McLain told the mob. "I shoot for that every year."

Somebody asked him about Bob Gibson.

"If he pitches the first game, we'll meet," said McLain. "It's not an obsession with me. He's got his job, I've got mine."

McLain went out to the field for his usual 10 minutes of throwing.

Dizzy Dean went to observe.

"I'm getting more publicity now with Denny winning thirty than I did when I won thirty," said Dean.

John Sain was tutoring McLain.

"See how you'll look in thirty-four years," said Sain, pointing to the ample Dizzy Dean.

"I won't be alive in thirty-four years," said McLain, "because of this man."

McLain tapped his fingers against Mayo Smith.

There was a ball game to be played tonight. Earl Wilson pitched, hit his seventh home run and picked a runner off second base. He beat the A's, 3–0. As the game started, Denny McLain drove the white Cadillac with his name written on the door from the parking lot. He went home to seclusion. He went to sleep without trouble.

Baltimore continued its slump. The magic number was five.

SEPTEMBER 14

As the reporters and TV cameramen swarmed on the field before today's ball game, which would be televised nationally, Jim Pagliaroni marched around with a placard on his back. The A's catcher carried this message:

DOBSON GOING FOR NO. 12 TODAY.

Chuck Dobson would be Denny McLain's pitching rival this afternoon.

McLain arose at 10:30 and had two eggs and sausages for breakfast. At 11:05 he had a business meeting with the people from Hammond Organ. "I've got to be something to have a business meeting on the day I'm going for thirty," McLain said.

At noon Denny and his brother Tim left the house in Beverly Hills, Michigan, for the drive to Tiger Stadium.

He was surrounded as he put on his white home uniform with the Old English D on the chest. He was surrounded as he took batting practice. He was surrounded as he returned to the clubhouse.

"You bet I'm going to ask for a hundred thousand dollars," he said.

"No, I didn't like the thing in *Life*. If I ever catch the photographer, I'll kill him."

Finally he asked to be left alone. He picked up a newspaper and walked to the back of the clubhouse toward the bathroom and Bill Behm's training room. Joe Falls had written a column in this morning's paper telling of all the things that could be purchased for $100,000.

Dizzy Dean went with him for a private chat.

"He tried to pretend he wasn't nervous, and he might have been right," said Dean, who was writing special articles for the *News*. "He got the paper and sat on the rubbin' table. Then he started talkin' about what he could do with one hundred thousand dollars."

Denny McLain finally walked through the clubhouse, picked up his glove and jacket and went out to warm up.

"I'll tell you, it's exciting," said Sandy Koufax.

There were 44,088 people in Tiger Stadium, among them David Eisenhower and Julie Nixon in a box near where Denny warmed up. When he finished and was ready to start his quest for number thirty, McLain gave a baseball to David Eisenhower.

It was runless until the fourth inning when Reggie Jackson tagged Denny for a two-run homer into the right-field seats. Norm Cash hit a three-run homer to put Denny in front, 3–2, in the bottom of the inning.

The A's tied it in the fifth, and Jackson put them back ahead, 4–3, with his second homer in the sixth. That score remained until the bottom of the ninth. Diego Segui, the A's reliever, kept turning the Tigers back.

Once more Mayo Smith was forced to pinch-hit for McLain with him behind in a ball game. Al Kaline was the pinch hitter.

Denny sat down on the bench and waited and watched.

Kaline walked, and Smith signaled Dick McAuliffe to bunt. Mac fouled two pitches away and then swung. He hit a pop foul which third baseman Sal Bando caught in front of the dugout. McLain grimaced.

Then Mickey Stanley ripped a single into center field and Kaline raced to third. He was the potential tying run. The A's brought their infield up. Jim Northrup bounced the ball to Danny Cater, the first baseman. Cater grabbed the ball in his mitt and threw home ahead of the onrushing Kaline.

The throw was high and off the plate, and Kaline bounced into the catcher, Dave Duncan. The throw sailed past Duncan. Kaline crawled on hands and knees back to the plate and touched it. The score was tied.

Stanley ran to third base. Now Willie Horton came up.

Bob Kennedy, the A's manager, brought his outfield in close for the possible play on Stanley at the plate.

Dizzy Dean, at the rail by the third base dugout in a pack of writers and photographers, mumbled, "Ain't this thrillin'."

McLain stood up in the dugout and Kaline stood next to him.

Horton took a called strike from Segui.

"Only a fly ball," pleaded Willie.

He fouled off the next pitch and the next one. He was behind on the count, 0–2. The next two pitches were out of the strike zone and the count was 2–2.

The crowd was standing, and Horton swung at the next pitch.

He hit the fly ball, deep, deep to left field. Jim Gosger, in left field, backpedaled, but it was useless. The ball landed beyond him, and Mickey Stanley ran in and touched home plate.

Denny McLain had won number thirty.

He danced from the dugout with Al Kaline's arms entwined about him. McLain hugged Stanley and then he hugged Horton and then his teammates picked him up and carried him to the dugout.

Dizzy Dean clutched at him and McLain said, "Thanks, Big Diz."

Sandy Koufax grabbed him and interviewed him on national TV. "Thank you, thank you," he said to congratulations. The people screamed and shrieked, and finally Denny was led to the clubhouse. The audience was around his locker.

"When Al got on, I knew I had a chance," said the 30-game winner. "I didn't say anything in the dugout."

"Excited?" asked a writer.

"Sure, I'm excited, but I'm going to be more excited in a few days," said the 30-game winner.

Outside, the old ball park was rocking with the noise. Thousands were packed in the grandstand around third base behind the dugout. These were the people, the ones McLain

Camera 5 (Lester Sloan)

Denny McLain tells Sandy Koufax, Dizzy Dean and a nation-wide television audience how it feels to win 30 games.

had criticized in May when he discussed the Detroit fans, the worst, they don't deserve a pennant . . . some of them.

"We want Denny, we want Denny, we want Denny," they yelled and yelled and yelled.

Outside the clubhouse door other fans stampeded, yelling for Denny. Hal Middlesworth, the PR man, pushed through the audience around McLain.

"There's no way these people will go away until we take him out there," said Middlesworth. An honor guard of ushers led McLain through the dark tunnel into the dugout and up the steps to the field.

The people cheered and yelled Denny's name. He stood there and waved back and murmured, "Thank you, thank you."

"Those people," said McLain. "It's fantastic. They're the best fans in the world."

McLain was led back into the dugout and to the clubhouse.

"No, I wasn't nervous," he said.

"When did you really start thinking of thirty?"

"When I won number one," said McLain, and the grin was impish. "Really, when I won number fifteen."

"What about Jackson's homers?"

"What do you expect in Jim Campbell's Tiger Stadium?" said McLain. "We've been after him for years to put a screen in front of the lower stands. I hate this park."

"One hundred thousand dollars?"

"I want a hundred thousand, and that's what I'm going to get," said the 30-game winner.

"What are you going to do tonight?"

"I'm going home and have a couple of cool ones," said the 30-game winner. "Then my wife and I will think of something."

It was Last Licks Victory Number Twenty-six. The magic number was four. The Tigers had another of those five-game winning streaks.

SEPTEMBER 15

Mickey Lolich hopped aboard his motorcycle and zoomed down the highway toward Tiger Stadium. He was going to pitch for victory number fifteen.

He got it with his second straight shutout over the A's, 13–0. Jim Northrup and Bill Freehan hit two home runs each. Willie Horton hit one, number thirty-six.

It was the Tigers' sixth straight victory, and the Orioles lost again. The magic number was halved to two.

Even Mayo Smith did not shudder when somebody threw a packet of "Meet Me in St. Looie" bumper stickers on his desk. The Cardinals won the National League pennant today.

"This has been an enjoyable year," said Smith. "We accomplished a lot this year. I mean in team spirit. We've never had it like this before, I mean spirit from some individuals."

SEPTEMBER 16

Tonight could be the night.

The Yankees were in town with a ten-game winning streak while the Tigers had won six straight.

There was amusement among the Tigers because of what Joe Cronin had done earlier in the day. The league president fired two umpires, Al Salerno and Bill Valentine, because they were attempting to organize an umpires' association. "Incompetence," was Cronin's reason, and it made Dick McAuliffe chuckle.

Mickey Lolich was on a
winning cycle.

UPI

John Hand, the clubhouse man, had 108 bottles of champagne stashed away on ice just in case.

The Tigers won without trouble. Norm Cash hit a home run and a single and drove in five runs.

The bullpen rested again as John Hiller pitched the tenth straight complete game. He handled the Yankees, 9–1.

The Tigers were positive of a tie for the pennant. They trooped into the clubhouse and watched the pro football game in St. Louis on TV. They waited while the Orioles played the Red Sox to a conclusion in Boston. Finally the score came, the Orioles winners, 8–1. The bright TV lights were turned off and everybody went home to wait.

The Tigers did not win the pennant tonight. They would have to wait at least until tomorrow night's game with the Yankees. But they had cut the magic number to one.

SEPTEMBER 17

Al Kaline, the noted bench rider, had a vision today.

"I feel I'm going to do something to win the pennant tonight," Kaline said to his wife, Louise. "I don't know what, but I have that feeling."

The people came to the ball park, baseball fans. They came alone or in twos, 46,512 of them. Some left their parcels at the gates as they were checked by the guards. They had been waiting twenty-three years. Al Kaline had been waiting sixteen.

In the clubhouse, Joe Sparma was shirtless. He spoke to Denny McLain. "Set up a card table for the two of us," suggested Sparma. The bullpen had not been needed for 10 games. Sparma hadn't pitched in 15 days. He hadn't been a winning pitcher since July 25.

Earl Wilson got up from his corner locker and went out to warm up. He threw and his shoulder hurt. He threw again and it hurt some more. Wilson went to tell Mayo Smith. Smith nodded and went looking for Pat Dobson.

"Earl's hurt his arm," said Smith. "I want you to pitch tonight."

"As long as you want me in the bullpen in the World Series I'd just as soon stay there and be ready if you need me in relief," said Dobson. "I'd rather not start."

"Joe, Joe Sparma," yelled a fan into the dugout, "how about an autograph?"

Sparma got up to accommodate the fan.

"Joe," said Mayo Smith upon hearing the fan yell the name, "how much did you throw tonight?"

"About fifteen minutes," said Sparma.

"Can you start tonight?" asked Smith.

"I can," said Sparma.

"Just go in and throw as hard as you can as long as you can," said Smith.

Sparma picked up his glove and walked to the warmup mound to throw to Hal Naragon, the bullpen coach.

Boo . . . boo . . . boo . . . the 46,512 greeted the pitcher who'd said he'd been humiliated just a month ago. "We want Wilson," bellowed a leather-lung from the third base side. Sparma continued to warm up.

"Let's go, Joe, let's go, Joe," the crowd suddenly changed its chant.

Horace Clarke led off with a sharp single and Jake Gibbs hit a hard drive to Mickey Stanley in center. The Yankees were teeing off on Sparma.

Out in the bullpen, Pat Dobson came out of the enclosure and started to warm up.

Mickey Mantle beat out an infield single. The Yankees had two on with one out. But Roy White grounded to Dick Mc-

Auliffe, who started a rapid double play. Sparma was out of the jam.

He retired the Yankees in order in the second and again in the third. There were cheers when Sparma batted in the third.

In the fourth and fifth, Sparma again retired the Yankees three up and three down.

On the scoreboard the Red Sox had a 2–0 lead over the Orioles. Here it was 0–0.

Bill Freehan singled off Stan Bahnsen leading off the Tigers' fifth. He went to second on a grounder. Sparma came up with two outs, and there was another burst of applause.

The pitcher rapped the ball into center field to single home Freehan with the first run of the game.

In the sixth, Sparma had retired 14 straight Yankees when he walked Bahnsen. Dobson again came out of the bullpen dugout and started warming up. Sparma again got out of trouble.

He still led, 1–0, when he came to bat in the eighth and had given the Yankees but one hit since the first.

The crowd of 46,512 stood up and gave him a tremendous ovation.

The scoreboard showed the Red Sox still 2–0 ahead of Baltimore in the eighth when the Yankees came to bat in the ninth.

The Tigers' bullpen emptied as the excess relief pitchers went to the dugout to await the next three outs. All the Tigers in the dugout were standing. Only Mayo Smith remained seated on his special platform, arms folded across his chest.

Three more outs.

Charlie Smith led off with a pinch single, and Sparma then got the next two outs. Dick Howser, running for Smith, was at second. Gibbs came to the plate.

At 9:58 P.M., Pete Sark, a Flint radio man, yelled into the press box that it was all over at Boston.

The scoreboard atop the center-field bleachers remained:

BALT 0
8
BOST 2

Only a few knew what had happened. The news from Boston came over the ticker into the broadcast booth. But Jim Campbell asked that Ernie Harwell refrain from announcing the score. He did not want the fans suddenly climbing over the fences and rushing onto the field and causing forfeiture of the game to the Yankees.

Sparma continued pitching and Gibbs singled to center. Howser scored and the game was tied, 1–1. Sparma then struck out Mickey Mantle.

The Tigers came to bat in the bottom of the ninth. The 46,512 fans, oblivious to the result in Boston, shrieked for another rally.

The phone rang in the Tigers' dugout. Freehan picked it up. It was Howard Stitzel, the broadcast engineer, calling from the radio booth.

"Boston beat Baltimore," said Stitzel.

Freehan carefully hung up the receiver and went over to inform Mayo Smith. The Tigers whispered the news among each other. The fans who could see into the dugout saw no emotion, nothing . . . nothing but all the Tigers now sitting down and Mayo Smith standing.

Charley Creedon, the traveling secretary, walked down the tunnel and to the inside steps of the dugout and confirmed the report.

The scoreboard still indicated it was the ninth inning in Boston with the Orioles behind, 2–0.

Steve Hamilton, a left-hander, came in to relieve for the Yankees in the bottom of the ninth. He struck out Jim Northrup for one out. Willie Horton grounded to third for the second out. Two outs, none on, score 1–1.

"We'll have to put up the Orioles' score at the end of this inning, no matter," Jim Campbell told Hal Middlesworth.

Smith, going by the guidebook, sent up a pinch hitter for Norm Cash.

Al Kaline walked to the plate. He worked a walk out of Hamilton. Freehan singled to left. Mayo Smith sent up Jim Price to bat for Ray Oyler. But Lindy McDaniel was brought in to pitch for the Yankees. Mayo countered by sending up Gates Brown, the celebrated pinch batsman, to hit for Price. Brown walked to load the bases.

The scoreboard still showed the incomplete score at Boston.

Don Wert came up. McDaniel pitched high for a ball and then got a called strike over. Wert fouled off the next pitch.

McDaniel pitched again and Wert swung. The ball was lined sharply to right field. Al Kaline ran as hard as he could toward home plate and touched it with his spiked shoe. It was 10:18 P.M.

The Tigers, champions for 20 minutes, had won the American League pennant . . . in their own fashion, Last Licks Victory Number Twenty-seven.

The scoreboard then flashed the final 2–0 loss for Baltimore.

The players poured from the dugout and pummeled Kaline, and they pummeled Don Wert, who had a .198 batting average. They pummeled Mayo Smith.

And the people came, hurdling the fences, pouring from the grandstands in their ecstasy. They scampered around the outfield, retreating when a fireworks display was set off. SOCKIT TO 'EM, TIGERS were the words written by the fireworks.

It was over. The Tigers had won the pennant—after twenty-three years. The people came in multitudes, people turned into an uncontrolled crowd by a baseball pennant.

They flattened metal box seats and pulled down the left-field screen and bent the fence in right. Strips of sod were pulled from the playing field. There were blacks and whites

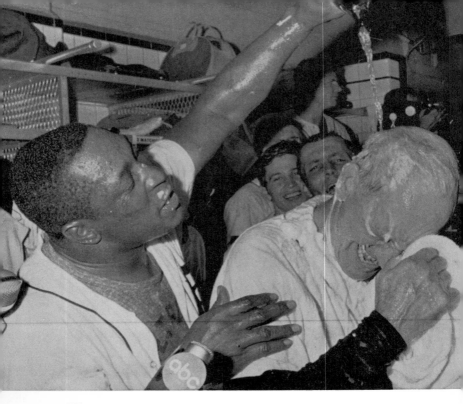

Gates Brown gives Mayo Smith a champagne shampoo after the Tigers win the American League flag.

in the throng. On the pitcher's mound a special cop pirouetted, swinging a billy club against the horde of souvenir hunters.

The Tigers battled their way back to the clubhouse as the mob pressed on the dugout and was repulsed by the police.

Horns blasted throughout the city, and in the clubhouse John Hand opened the cases of champagne.

The people inside the clubhouse acted just like the people outside on the field. The champagne was used for pouring on one another's heads. Denny McLain went around spraying shaving cream on his teammates, on owner John Fetzer, on Mayo Smith, on the baseball writers.

Fetzer was tossed into the whirlpool bath in his blue suit. Jim Campbell went in and Mayo Smith was thrown in, splashing in his baseball uniform. Some writers and TV men were thrown in. Mickey Stanley dove in on his own.

Al Kaline struggled with a bottle of champagne.

"After all these years and I can't get the damned cork out," he said.

And Joe Sparma stood happily, enjoying the ceremony. He had won, and for the first time since May had pitched nine innings. He was part of it.

"I won this game for the people who had faith in me," said Sparma, "and for my wife."

Sparma turned to Dobson.

"How come he didn't come for you?" asked Sparma.

"He came for me," replied Dobson. "I told him I didn't want to pitch."

Smith was flushed from the whirlpool and went dripping into his office.

"We'd wanted to win it this way, for the fans," said Smith, "even though we knew Baltimore lost. We'd done it this way all year.

"I'm glad two guys that had it rough all year did it for us. Sparma was under duress because he didn't have a chance to warm up. I was going to go with Sparma as long as I could and then with Dobson. And Wert came through when we wanted a hit.

"Is there more champagne?" Smith turned to John Hand. "Get me some. I might stay here all night.

"Al Kaline—as great as he played all these years, never a pennant winner. This is what you do as a little kid, dream of it. Playing in the World Series, managing in it. I waited for mine for thirty-six years.

"I want to tell you what a great team we've got. The spirit. Norm Cash came to me and said, 'Don't feel bad if you want Kaline to hit for me.' This is typical of this team. Two years ago they were individuals."

Denny McLain, covered with champagne and shaving soap, burst into the room.

"I want to sit here," said McLain. He plopped into Smith's swivel chair and put his feet on Mayo's desk.

"Now we need a Hammond organ here," said Manager McLain. "We've got to pitch the kids. I can't start tomorrow. I've got a headache. The air is circling.

"I'll tell you if I ever have this office, I'll have it air-conditioned. One hundred thousand dollars isn't enough to have this job. A half million. If you win, you don't get credit. If you lose, you get blamed."

"This guy was fabulous," said Smith. "But this wasn't a one-man team. You don't win pennants that way."

Willie Horton came in.

"Denny, we did it," yelled Horton, and suddenly he was aware of where McLain was seated. "You get out of his chair. You get out of his chair."

McLain got out of the chair. Earl Wilson sat down in it.

John Fetzer, soaked through his suit, walked in and wrapped his arms around his manager.

"Mayo, it was great," said the owner. "It was more than winning the pennant. It was for Detroit. This may save Detroit."

Outside in the main area of the clubhouse Bill Freehan told how he'd answered the phone in the middle of the ninth. He was the first Tiger to know that the pennant had been won, before the phony tension in the bottom of the ninth.

"Hell, no, there was no eruption on the bench," said Freehan. "We wanted to come from behind and win because that's the way we've been doing it all year. We didn't come from behind tonight, but we did come from a tie."

Jim Price, the number two catcher, was sprawled in the corner, out.

"Get up, get up," screamed Freehan standing over Price, who had a faint smile on his lips. "Get up, you've got to catch tomorrow night."

Mickey Lolich, the floppy-eared, potbellied left-hander, spoke of his season—exile to the bullpen and then a return to starting to aid in the pennant drive.

"You know Mickey Lolich," he said, "he always seems to come along when he has to."

Denny McLain was asked about the Cardinals.

"I don't want to just beat them," said the 30-game winner. "I want to humiliate them."

"I had a feeling today was it," said Al Kaline. "I was sitting on the bench and Wayne Comer said to me, 'You're going to win the game.' I told him I'd had that feeling all day."

Now Mayo Smith had to find a spot to play Kaline in the World Series.

There was pandemonium all the way from the ball park along Michigan Avenue to downtown a mile away. Blacks and whites joined hands and rode on hoods of cars. It was bedlam.

Outside the Lindell AC, the town's sports hangout, proprietor Jimmy Butsicaris had to screen the entrants, and the rest formed a cheering mob outside. One by one the Tigers arrived—McLain, Sparma, Horton, Wilson, Wert, Freehan and the others—and walked behind the bar to the cheers of the people inside.

SEPTEMBER 18

Today's game with the Yankees was rained out, which was a good thing.

SEPTEMBER 19

Willie Horton was appointed acting manager for this afternoon's game with the Yankees. He decided to break in with a 30-game winner and started Denny McLain.

McLain was willing.

"I'm trying to get back into shape after these last two days," he said. "I'll bet I gained ten pounds since we won the pennant. Everytime I turned around somebody was offering me a meal. I'll bet there are more half-eaten meals around town."

Mayo Smith said Denny would pitch to keep himself in his normal rotation, maybe five or six innings. It was only for exercise.

The acting manager, Horton, took the lineup cards out to the plate. They went through the usual pregame rigmarole about the ground rules and such.

Horton returned to the dugout and assumed a stance near Mayo's platform.

"I don't want you around," Horton told Smith.

"Where do you want me to go?" said Smith, leaving for the far end of the dugout.

McLain pitched through the fifth, then the sixth, then the seventh, by which time Mayo again was managing. Norm Cash hit two homers and McLain was coasting. In the eighth, Mickey Mantle came up for what the 9,000 customers believed would be his last appearance in Detroit. Mantle had 534 home runs in his career. He needed one more to break his tie with Jimmy Foxx and become number three man on the all-time list behind Babe Ruth and Willie Mays.

The people stood up to give Mantle a thunderous ovation. Then they started that rhythmic clapping, beseeching Mantle to hit one.

Only Denny McLain knows whether he intentionally fed Mickey Mantle that 535th home run.

Camera 5 (Lester Sloan)

McLain got two strikes on Mantle and then Mickey fouled the next pitch off. As McLain rubbed up the new ball, Mantle moved his hand over the plate about letters-high. He was requesting a pitch right there.

Denny threw it there, and Mantle hit the ball high into the right-field seats for number 535. The crowd stood cheering, and as he ran around third base, Mantle yelled thanks to McLain.

The Tigers jumped onto the steps of their dugout and applauded Mantle's home run against them. The ball was retrieved and thrown to the dugout and Mantle came out to get it. He saluted McLain with it.

McLain won number thirty-one by a 6–2 score and again was surrounded in the clubhouse.

"Mickey was your idol, wasn't he?" said a writer.

"He's still my idol," said the 31-game winner.

"I'd like to have that ball. I'd like to see what it looks like."

Everybody laughed.

"I think you guys think I did that on purpose," said McLain with a twinkle. "Then baseball would be crooked and I'd be investigated.

"He hit a perfect pitch. He hit a helluva pitch. Oh, I was happy he hit a home run. But I did not let him hit it."

"Oh?"

"My biggest thrill of the game was when Mickey hit that home run," said McLain. "I felt like a fan. But I did not let him hit it."

"Thirty-two?"

"It's not a necessary thing with me," said the 31-game winner. "You know, I'm glad we don't win pennants every night."

"When the fans cheered me here today," said Mickey Mantle, "cold chills went all over me. Then Denny came in and told the catcher, 'I'm going to throw only fastballs,' I think. He did out of the goodness of his heart. I want to thank Denny. I had the feeling he let me hit it."

SEPTEMBER 29

Now Mayo Smith had one dilemma before the Tigers went into the World Series: how to get Al Kaline into the lineup. The Tigers had finished the formalities of the American League schedule today with a 103–59 record. The Orioles, killed off in the weekend series a month ago, straggled in a dozen games behind the Tigers.

After clinching the pennant, the blithe Tigers had extended their winning streak to 11 games. The bullpen continued unused for 13 games as each pitcher finished everything he started.

Denny McLain twice was unable to win number thirty-two, losing once to Baltimore. McLain wound up the season with a 31–6 record, the first 31-game winner since Lefty Grove in 1931.

At Baltimore the Tigers gave the Orioles a farewell memory. Behind, 3–1, in the ninth, Gates Brown hit a three-run homer for Last Licks Victory Number Twenty-eight.

The Tigers completed the season with 40 victories in games in which they were either behind or tied as late as the seventh inning.

Their attendance for the year was 2,031,847, marking the first time the Tigers ever drew more than two million.

Smith briefly employed Gates Brown and rookie Bob Christian as first basemen. Eight different players handled the position during the season, which started with Mickey Stanley there on opening day.

Soon after the Tigers clinched the pennant, Smith had called Kaline into his office.

"I guess you know what a tough decision I have to make for the Series," Smith said. "I just don't know what to do about it."

"I know what kind of pressure you're under," said Kaline, "but it was the kids who won the pennant. I wouldn't feel badly if you played them in the Series and not me."

Kaline was practically volunteering to serve as a benchwarmer for the World Series, to yield to the young outfielders. Smith was moved by the gesture.

"I appreciate it, Al," he said. "Maybe there's a possibility you can play third base. I'll think about it."

The Tigers had to go into Baltimore for a series that once loomed as critical but now was meaningless. There Smith again talked with Kaline.

"Keep playing right field," Smith said.

He decided to experiment with center fielder Mickey Stanley at shortstop. Stanley played the position in the final six games while Smith mulled about what to do, and watched. Could Stanley get the grounder right at him? Could he go to his right into the hole? Could he throw from there? How did he handle the double play?

As late as yesterday, Smith had reservations. Then, watching Stanley in today's final game, Smith decided to start him at short in the Series.

"You're going to play right field," he told Kaline, "for the first game, at least. We'll see how Mickey does at shortstop."

Never before had a manager entered the World Series with such a bold, experimental gamble.

"I'm not being sentimental, this is no gesture to get Kaline in the World Series," Smith declared. "I'm trying to get an extra bat in against the Cardinals."

Managers certainly had gambled before in the World Series. They had taken pitchers from the bullpen or from deep in the rotation and pitched them in the first game. But never had a manager taken an outstanding outfielder and made him a shortstop for the World Series. Mickey Stanley had not committed an error all season as the Tigers' center fielder. But there was no reliable hitting at shortstop.

It was a chance, and it solved the dilemma.

Al Kaline, after sixteen years, had to play in the World Series. Smith, as manager of the Tigers, owed that to Kaline. It was sentimental in that respect. But Kaline was still an excellent ballplayer, the Tigers' best all around.

To get him—and his bat—into the World Series, Smith was weakening two positions in the field. Stanley was a risk at a foreign position, the hardest of all to play. The Tigers could lose in the Series because of a misplay at shortstop. Northrup, better in right field, could not equal Stanley in center. The Series could also be lost by a misplay in center. But Northrup would play there in three days when Denny McLain pitched against Bob Gibson in the Great Confrontation.

Mayo the Maneuverer was breaking up the lineup of the June surge which put the Tigers in control of the pennant race.

"I hope I can just be adequate," said Stanley. "That's all Mayo wants from me. I know I'll be tight, but then I'd feel the same way in center field for my first Series game.

"I only hope somebody hits that first ground ball to me in a hurry."

Smith made one other decision. He made Eddie Mathews eligible for the World Series and dropped John Wyatt from the roster.

Now all that mattered was McLain vs. Gibson in the most celebrated pitchers' battle of the age.

SEPTEMBER 30

This afternoon the Tigers flew via charter to St. Louis for their first World Series since 1945.

OCTOBER 1

Denny McLain was awake early and dressed and went to Busch Stadium down near the Mississippi River. Bob Gibson was already there.

McLain put on his gray road baseball suit and walked through the tunnel and into the third base dugout. He climbed the steps and went onto the field. The audience followed him across.

At the first base dugout they shook hands—the 31-game winner and the pitcher whose 1.12 earned-run average was the lowest in fifty years.

McLain spoke first.

"I'm Denny McLain, nice to meet you."

"Thanks, I'm Bob Gibson."

It was that casual, that brief. There was no grudge because, as both explained, how could there be when they had just met?

"It's not a match between two pitchers, but a game between two teams," said Gibson.

"This thing between Gibson and me has been blown all out of proportion," said McLain.

But if the Series went seven games, they could expect to oppose each other three times.

"I think I'll be more nervous on opening night in Las Vegas," said McLain.

The Series had not started, but Mayo Smith already had been second-guessed from coast to coast. Mickey Stanley was scrutinized practicing at shortstop with Ray Oyler alongside, his personal hurry-up tutor.

There was the specter of Lou Brock, whose feet had stolen seven bases a year ago in the World Series against the Red

Sox. It would be the responsibility of the pitchers to keep Brock close and Bill Freehan's to throw him out. A player such as Brock could turn the Series to the Cardinals, away from the Tigers.

And ignored and sitting alone again at his locker was Mickey Lolich.

"It's like starting the season," said Lolich to a single reporter. "This might be the only season I'd say I'd like to win only two games."

On the eve of the first World Series game, Denny McLain entered the Gashouse Lounge at the Tigers' hotel, the Sheraton-Jefferson. He was with Sharyn and several other

Antagonists in the Great Confrontation: Denny McLain and Bob Gibson.

UPI

Denny tuned up on the organ on the eve of the first game.

Tiger couples. Coaxed, McLain went over to the Hammond organ and entertained.

"I did about an hour and twenty minutes," he said. "Me and Northrup. He was doing a little bit of everything, singing.

"If there was a ten o'clock curfew, I missed it."

A photographer took a picture of McLain at the organ—and even before the Series started, Denny was vulnerable to criticism.

But the teammates who were with him testified McLain and they were gone and in their rooms before midnight.

OCTOBER 2

Denny McLain was awakened at 8:30 in his hotel room by the telephone. His caller was Frank Scott, his agent.

"He called about money," said the 31-game winner. "The show must go on, but the money comes first."

Bob Gibson was the show.

Mickey Stanley played shortstop professionally. He threw out Lou Brock for the first out in the bottom of the first. Stanley got two hits off Gibson. He earned another day at shortstop.

Al Kaline got a double, and three other times Gibson struck him out.

McLain had difficulty with his control and his fastball was not fast. He battled Gibson into the fourth. Then McLain walked two batters and Mike Shannon and Julian Javier singled. The Cardinals scored three runs.

In the sixth, Mayo Smith used a pinch hitter and took McLain from the game.

The Great Confrontation did not match its ballyhoo. Gibson was great. He had 14 strikeouts entering the ninth. Then

Tiger Norm Cash had reason to be disgusted: He was Bob Gibson's 16th strikeout victim.

after Stanley singled, he struck out Kaline, Norm Cash and Willie Horton.

He struck out 17 Tigers, a World Series record, and won 4–0 with a five-hitter. Getting Cash in the ninth was the strikeout that broke the former record.

"I knew when to take advantage of a situation," said Cash, who had been given $150 to appear on television as the record-breaking victim.

"It was better than hitting a little dribbler."

Mayo Smith told the Tigers the obvious.

" 'We've been behind before,' I told them," he said. " 'It takes four to win it.' "

Tonight McLain returned to the Gashouse Lounge. After pleading by the organist and applause from the audience, McLain went up and entertained on the organ again. Denny took the microphone in his hand when they asked him to sing, too.

"Mr. Gibson was super today," he said. "I don't even feel bad about getting beat. He pitched one helluva ball game. I can't sing and I don't pitch too well, either."

OCTOBER 3

Mayo Smith had changed his mind about his pitcher in today's second game. Originally he planned on Earl Wilson. Mickey Lolich was a better pitcher in Detroit than on the road. But Wilson had those seven home runs and the fences were much closer in Detroit. With that reasoning Mayo saved Wilson for the third game at Tiger Stadium.

"His bat is a big factor there," Smith said on the field before the second game. "He gives us another bat and we need it. That's why he'll pitch there and Lolich is going here today."

The Tigers had been jittery in the first game. They finally admitted this fact.

Today Lolich had problems in the first inning. Julian Javier singled with one out and Lolich walked Curt Flood. But Al Kaline made a long run and caught Orlando Cepeda's foul fly. Then he ran the other way and caught Mike Shannon's liner to right center. Lolich escaped.

With one out in the second, Willie Horton tagged Nellie Briles for a towering home run to left. For the first time in the Series there was some spark in the Tigers' dugout. Lolich came to bat in the third with one out. The motorcycle aficionado was not another bat in the lineup, as Mayo would say.

So Mickey socked the ball near the foul line and into the left-field seats. It was his first home run as a professional. He began the 360-foot journey around the bases and at first missed the bag.

"Hey, come back," yelled Wally Moses, the coach.

Lolich retreated two steps and touched first.

"I'm not used to this sort of thing," said Lolich.

His lead was 2–0. Norm Cash homered in the fifth and the Tigers scored twice more. Lolich had some trouble in the sixth, started by Lou Brock, who walked and stole second. He scored, but Lolich escaped danger when Mickey Stanley started a double play on a grounder to shortstop.

With the lead 6–1 in the seventh, Smith made his defensive realignment as planned. He moved Stanley to center, Jim Northrup to left and kept Al Kaline in right. Ray Oyler went in to play short. Horton had to leave and fumed in the dugout.

"I want my three best arms out there when we're ahead like that in the late innings," the maneuverer explained to the writers.

But he had not told this to Horton, and Willie was irked.

"I didn't like it a bit," said Horton. "I played out there all year and I'm not that bad a left fielder. He might have said something to me about it before he did it."

Lolich was under medication and did not expect to survive

the entire game. But he did and won, 8–1, and the Series was evened. Their only problem today was Brock. He stole two bases and had three in the two games.

After the game, Lolich stood in the interview room beneath Busch Stadium and revealed why he did not expect to pitch nine innings.

"I had a boil on my . . . my whatchamacallit," Lolich said with a grin to a room full of writers from across the country. They immediately thought of ways how they'd write that.

"I was groggy and afraid I'd have no energy late in the game," said Lolich.

They flew back to Detroit with restored confidence and had a welcoming reception from the fans at Metro Airport.

OCTOBER 4

Mayo Smith called Willie Horton into the manager's office at Tiger Stadium and shut the door. Mayo explained to his left fielder the defensive strategy he intended to use in this World Series.

"You can cover as much ground as Northrup to catch a fly," Smith explained, "but my decision is based on throwing and there is a difference."

Willie nodded.

"I wasn't really that mad," Horton said after he left the office. "He's the manager and I understand he has to make decisions."

The door closed again, and this time Denny McLain was inside. Among the matters discussed was organ recitals in the lounge at the hotel in St. Louis.

Tonight McLain and Bob Gibson taped a TV special with Bob Hope.

"It took me eleven cuts to say *epitomize*," said McLain. "Bob Gibson epitomizes American sportsmanship.

"People tried to make out we're at each other's throats. We're not."

After the taping, McLain loaded Gibson into the white Cadillac with *Denny McLain* written on the doors. He gave Gibson a ride to the Twenty Grand, a Detroit nightclub.

"He's a pretty nice guy," said McLain.

OCTOBER 5

The first World Series in Detroit in twenty-three years . . .

The nearby parking lot operators boosted their prices five-fold to as high as $10. The ticket holders rode buses and cabs, and the nearby parking lots were virtually empty.

There was an electricity in the city. The city government had painted tiger heads in orange and white every several feet from downtown out Michigan Avenue to the ball park.

Billboards welcomed visitors and exhorted the Tigers: SHUFFLE THE CARDS, or told the world: IT AIN'T IN THE CARDS.

All the disc jockeys featured a new tune on their shows, "Go Get 'em, Tigers," which started with a sultry female growl.

The people came to the ball park, 53,634 of them. Most were not the people who had been there a year ago when the Tigers lost the pennant. Or on September 17 when they won the pennant. But this is what happens at a World Series, when half or more of the tickets are distributed to special people or special groups.

There was hardly a boo.

On the field before the ball game Denny McLain made a prediction.

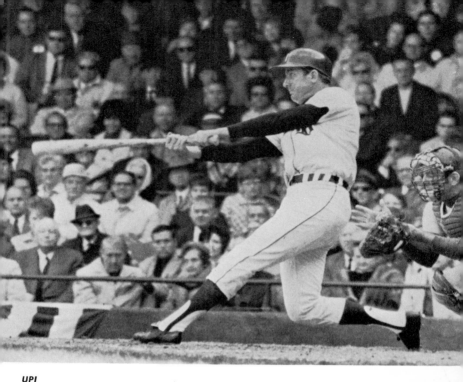

UPI

With one man on base, Al Kaline hit a long one into the stands.

"Whoever wins today will win the Series," he said.

It was Earl Wilson's turn to pitch, another episode in the *Perils of Earl.*

In the third inning Al Kaline came to bat with Dick McAuliffe on base. Kaline had gotten three hits in the first two games at St. Louis. Mayo Smith's maneuvering to create a position for Kaline was thus far justified.

Kaline hit Ray Washburn's pitch into the left-field seats for a 2–0 lead. In right field the people there stood and applauded him when he returned to his position.

Wilson took the 2–0 lead into the fifth. The first batter he faced was Lou Brock. Brock had walked his first time up and singled the second time up. Both times Brock stole second. Now he singled again—and stole second for the third time.

Curt Flood came up. On the third pitch to Flood, Wilson appeared to skid off balance as he threw. Bill Freehan walked out to the mound after the next pitch.

"I could see something sort of buckle," Freehan said. "The next pitch he sort of eased down into it. I went out and said: 'Hey, you hurt yourself?' and Earl said, 'Yeah.' "

Wilson tried to continue, and Flood hit a double to score Brock with the Cards' first run. When Roger Maris walked, Mayo Smith took Wilson from the game and brought in Pat Dobson. Tim McCarver cracked a three-run homer to put the Cards ahead, 4–2. In the bottom of the fifth, Dick McAuliffe cut the Tigers' deficit to 4–3 with a homer.

But with Orlando Cepeda hitting another three-run homer in the seventh, the Cardinals won the game, 7–3. They led in the Series, 2–1, and Bob Gibson was scheduled again for tomorrow against Denny McLain.

"If I can come out of a game alive, I feel I've had a good day," Earl Wilson said sadly in front of his locker. "This is the sixth time this year I was hurt pitching.

"I can't say if I slipped or caught my spikes on the mound. But there was a sharp pain in my leg. I stayed in the game because invariably something like that would go away."

The Tigers were down again. They were shaken by Brock and his base-paths speed. They felt betrayed by their own park, where the Cardinals suddenly were transformed into a team with power.

"I think we're in bad shape if we lose Sunday's game," said the candid Al Kaline. "We've got to think we can beat Gibson."

Freehan had not yet gotten a hit in nine at-bats in the Series, and Brock had stolen six bases.

"I think he's been thrown out only eleven times this year, so he's been stealing on other people, too," said Freehan.

OCTOBER 6

The rain poured down, drenching the outfield, forming puddles on the canvas over the infield. Tiger Stadium was a lagoon. The baseball commissioner, William D. Eckert, the unknown soldier, stood in the muck and turned his eyes into the raindrops and looked for blue skies. It continued to rain.

There was a great TV audience to see a jewel of the national pastime, the Sunday World Series game. It was the day for Great Confrontation II between Bob Gibson and Denny McLain. This was baseball's Super Sunday.

Catcher in the rain: Bill Freehan awaits start of fourth game.

UPI

Commissioner Eckert ordered "Play ball," and after a 37-minute drying-out delay, the fourth game began in a mist.

Lou Brock hit McLain's second pitch into the center-field bleachers for a home run. The Cardinals scored another run in the first and two more in the third on Tim McCarver's triple and Mike Shannon's double. It started to pour again. Vice President Hubert Humphrey took shelter in a room beneath the grandstands.

The ground crew struggled to drag the infield over the diamond, and the people booed their efforts.

"Rain, rain, rain," chanted the people of Detroit as the TV cameras focused in on the raindrops.

A World Series game, once started, never has been stopped partway by weather. The Tigers' fans cheered the rain because their team was trailing and it was not yet a game that would count.

For 74 minutes the World Series waited for the rain to slacken. Then it slowed enough for Commissioner Eckert to command a resumption.

During the interval, McLain went to Mayo Smith and suggested he be removed because his shoulder bothered him. Mayo had Joe Sparma pitching when the game resumed.

In the fourth, Gibson struck a home run and Brock tripled and then scored. The Cards led, 6–0, and hoped only to get the game through the fifth inning, when it would count. To expedite matters, Orlando Cepeda was ordered to run for second so he could be thrown out stealing to end the fourth.

The Tigers attempted to stall, and the Cardinals attempted to hasten the lopsided game. The World Series had become a farce. The players sloshed around and deliberately attempted to make outs and the rain fell and the nation watched the incredible spectacle in its living rooms.

In the fifth, Julian Javier was caught stealing when he took off with pitcher Daryl Patterson still gripping the ball on the mound.

The umpires, shackled by the high command's orders, called

out both managers. They told Mayo and Red Schoendienst to knock off their respective stalling and speed-up.

The fourth World Series game was played to a nine-inning completion. Bob Gibson beat the Tigers for the second time, 10–1. In eighteen innings, Jim Northrup's home run today was the only run the Tigers could score against him.

Gibson had beaten Denny McLain a second time—and it was the Tigers who were being humiliated. The Cardinals controlled the Series, 3–1, and they were one victory from the World Championship.

The Tigers were unable to cope with Lou Brock, who had a double after his homer and triple. He stole his seventh base of the Series and tied his year-old record. Certainly now he would get his eighth steal and maybe more.

Shocked more than anything else, Denny McLain said to a reporter he felt he was finished for the Series.

The Tigers had been embarrassed in three of the four World Series games.

"A lot of people watching us must think we're a lousy club," said Al Kaline, who had got two hits off Gibson in the rain. "And we aren't."

Only twice before in history had a club trailing 3–1 rallied to win in a seven-game World Series—Pittsburgh in 1925, the Yankees in 1958. The Tigers could only reflect on all their comebacks this year. The Cardinals now were 8–1 favorites to win the World Series.

OCTOBER 7

This morning the national convention of the American Funeral Directors Association opened in Detroit. All summer this scheduled meeting of morticians, which would cause conflict for hotel rooms, had caused laughter.

Now the convention was starting ... with the Tigers near death.

"Wait until I get on that golf course. I'm going to give it hell," said Mayo Smith, standing on the field before game number five.

"Where's McLain?" asked a writer.

"McLain went to the doctor for a treatment," said Mayo.

"Will he be here?"

"I don't think he's going to play the organ someplace," responded Smith. "He's a member of the team."

"If you win, who'd you pitch in the sixth game?"

"Wilson threw today and he'd have another day off," said Smith. "Or Sparma. I feel reasonably sure Denny would pitch if there's a seventh game."

Lou Brock, who had eight hits and a .500 average and seven steals in the first four games, stood at the batting cage. A writer asked him how a ballplayer happened to get into the flower business on the side.

"Nobody asks Rockefeller why he got into the oil business," answered Brock.

"If the Series goes seven games, I'll pitch," said Denny McLain upon his arrival on the field. "That reporter took my quote the wrong way. I said I probably wouldn't pitch anymore, and he thought it was because of my arm. What I meant was the Cardinals had momentum and I thought ..."

Bill Freehan, hitless in 12 at-bats in the Series, walked by the cage carrying his bat.

"I'm going over to give Gibson my bat," said the moon-faced catcher with a big grin. "I'm going to say, 'Hey, you want this? You ain't hit it yet.'"

Such was the atmosphere as Mickey Lolich walked down to the left-field bullpen, the place where he had rediscovered his pitching talent in August. He began to warm up for his second start of the Series. His team had to win—or the Tigers' first World Series in twenty-three years was finished.

Lolich was interrupted in his warmup by "The Star-Spangled Banner." He turned toward center field and held his glove with the baseball in it in his left hand and held his cap in his right hand across his heart.

And suddenly everybody in the park stirred. The words were familiar, but the way they were sung was not. José Feliciano, a blind Puerto Rican pop singer, was singing his soul version of the national anthem. The ball park switchboard lighted up. Newspapers from New York to Los Angeles started receiving complaints. NBC stations across the nation started to get irate calls.

Then the ball game began with Lou Brock lining a double to left. Curt Flood singled Brock home and Orlando Cepeda hit a home run and Mickey Lolich was behind, 3–0, after facing four batters. Smith stuck with him.

In the third, Brock got another hit, a single, and as usual he sped for second on a steal attempt. This time Freehan gunned him down on a throw to Dick McAuliffe.

In the fourth, the Tigers whittled the deficit to 3–2 on Mickey Stanley's triple, Norm Cash's sacrifice fly, Willie Horton's triple and Jim Northrup's fluke single. Northrup's routine grounder to second suddenly rose and skipped over Julian Javier's head.

Brock got his third straight, a double, with one out in the fifth. Lolich again was in a jam. Javier singled the ball into left field and Brock took off.

In left field Horton gloved the ball buckle-high. Brock touched third and headed for home. Horton uncoiled the arm Smith had removed from the World Series three games before and unloosed the ball to the same appointed spot.

At home plate Bill Freehan flung his mask away and prepared to straddle the plate. He yelled nothing to Don Wert, the third baseman, who was the cutoff man. The silence was Freehan's signal to Wert to permit the throw to go through.

This is going to be close. The throw's good and he'll have to slide, were the thoughts rushing through Freehan's mind. Brock arrived perhaps an instant before the ball in Freehan's glove. But Brock did not slide. Freehan had the plate well blocked as he caught Horton's throw. He turned into Brock's body, the ball locked in his bare hand in the glove.

Behind home plate, umpire Doug Harvey unhesitatingly swept his right thumb in a vigorous downward arc. Lou Brock, the roadrunner, had been thrown out at home plate on a play he appeared to have beaten.

"Look at that, there are spike marks on the ground," Freehan said to Harvey. Harvey looked.

The Cards argued and Harvey supported his decision by saying, "He didn't touch the plate."

Lou Brock was nailed, standing up, at the plate by Bill Freehan.

UPI

TV ran the play at the plate over and over on the instant replay. But still nobody could be certain of anything more than that the Tigers still trailed by one run instead of two.

It remained Cards 3, Tigers 2, until the bottom of the seventh. Nellie Briles struck out Wert leading off the inning.

Lolich was the next batter. He looked at Mayo seated on the platform in the dugout. Smith motioned for him to go to the plate and bat—no pinch hitter even though the Tigers were behind.

Lolich looped the ball into right field for a single. The Cardinals brought in lefty Joe Hoerner to face McAuliffe. McAuliffe grounded the sidearm, left-handed pitch through an opening into right. Stanley walked to load the bases.

Now Al Kaline came up with the bat Mayo Smith had maneuvered for in the World Series. Kaline tapped the ball into right center field and Lolich scored and Mac scored and the Tigers were ahead. Cash singled home Stanley, and Lolich went out to pitch to the Cards in the eighth with a 5–3 lead.

Smith made his defensive adjustment with Ray Oyler entering at shortstop and Horton leaving the game.

Javier singled leading off the eighth. Then Curt Flood smashed the ball up the middle. McAuliffe went over and backhanded the bouncing ball with a stab. He forced Javier at second on a flip to Oyler. Instead of the tying run on with none out, the Cards had a runner at first with one out.

Lolich was able to survive. The Tigers won the fifth game, 5–3.

They were alive, and the evidence was in the spike marks at the edge of home plate, a footprint in the sand.

"They were two and a half inches from the plate," said Detective Freehan. "The umpire said if he'd have slid he would have been safe. I don't know. I say Brock's foot came short of the plate coming at my left foot.

"I was surprised he didn't slide. But I'm glad he didn't."

"I was safe," insisted Brock. "If I slide, he could come down with his knee and I wouldn't reach the plate. I tried to run through him."

The audience was now at Lolich's locker.

"I felt Mayo would hit for me, and I looked over and was surprised when he let me bat," said the rally starter who had yielded three runs before the game was five minutes old.

"The national anthem threw me off," explained Lolich. "I usually take twelve to thirteen minutes to warm up. Usually in Detroit I'm finished warming up and go to the mound, they play the national anthem, and the game starts.

"Today because it was the Series they played it early—right in the middle of my warmup. It took the guy three minutes to sing. Then the umps came out and started the game. I decided to rear back and throw as hard as I could. When I do that the ball comes in straight. That's what Brock hit."

"What'd you think of the national anthem?"

"It was sung a little different," responded Lolich.

"I let Lolich bat even though we were behind because we had two more shots," said Mayo Smith. "If Wert had gotten on, I'd have pinch-hit for Lolich. It was no gamble. This is what you're paid to do.

"As of now, it'll be Wilson or Sparma in the sixth game. Not McLain. But I can change my mind. It's like a woman's prerogative."

"The way we played the first couple of days in Detroit really hurt me," said game-winner Kaline. "My pride was hurt. I was representing the American League and I was embarrassed by it.

"I got a kick out of this hit. I'd rather be the one to do it than watching from the bench. I'm happy I'm doing as well as I'm doing in the Series. A lot of great players have had bad Series."

The Tigers had won another ball game with one of their late-inning rallies—the forty-first time. This time it meant there would be a sixth game back in St. Louis.

OCTOBER 8

The question on this off-day was whether Mayo Smith would exercise the managerial prerogative and change his mind. It seemed his safest course with the Tigers still scratching would be to pitch Denny McLain tomorrow. And if McLain won, Smith could use Mickey Lolich, his only Series winner, against Bob Gibson in the seventh game.

The Tigers worked out in Tiger Stadium this morning and McLain threw. Mayo had another of his chats, this one with McLain.

"How's your arm?" said Smith.

"I can pitch anytime you want me to," said Denny.

He had gone to Dr. Russell Wright's clinic yesterday, where he had taken his X ray treatments since August. This time he was given a shot of cortisone in his shoulder.

"My arm feels as good as it did all season," said McLain.

The Tigers departed for St. Louis with Smith saying he was undecided on his sixth-game pitcher.

"Wilson, Sparma or McLain," said Smith.

In St. Louis, McLain said privately he was the choice to start tomorrow. At 9:30 P.M., McLain walked through the lobby of the Sheraton-Jefferson and boarded the elevator and went to his room.

A few minutes later, the elevator came down and Mayo Smith stepped off into the lobby.

"I still haven't made up my mind," said Mayo. "I'll decide after I see them throw tomorrow."

He went out for dinner knowing almost certainly Denny McLain would pitch in the sixth game. The Tigers were down, 3–2, still at the brink—and McLain all summer had been the Tigers' best pitcher.

OCTOBER 9

Denny McLain was selected to pitch the most important game in his life today. Two hours before it was to begin he stood talking in the runway leading to the third base dugout at Busch Memorial Stadium.

The day he pitched to win 30, perhaps, contained more drama. But he would have had other chances to succeed there. If he failed today, he would have no other chance—and the accomplishment of 31 victories would be lessened by three losses in the World Series.

"I think I had a letdown myself after I won thirty and we won the pennant," said McLain. "To tell you the truth, I don't think I've gotten up for the Series yet.

"I think the only thing that has been damaged has been my pride. I think I have enough pride to overcome that."

Mayo Smith watched McLain throw when the Tigers arrived at the park. The cortisone shot had eased the pain and McLain threw hard. The manager then confirmed the decision he had made yesterday.

"Eight is a lot," said McLain to Jim Northrup in the clubhouse. "Get me eight."

In the first inning, it was apparent McLain was sharp again. He fired the baseball, placing it where he wanted.

In the second, Norm Cash worked a walk from Ray Washburn and Willie Horton lashed a double to left. Cash scored. Northrup struck out, and up came Bill Freehan, without a hit in the first five games, 0 for 16. Freehan dumped the ball into left field for his first hit and Horton scored. McLain had two of the eight he wanted.

He gave up a hit to Orlando Cepeda in the second. But Mickey Stanley, still Mayo's shortstop, started a double play to get the Tigers out of the inning.

The reception was grand for Jim Northrup after he hit a bases-loaded homer.

The Tigers' third began with Washburn walking Dick McAuliffe. Stanley singled and Al Kaline singled in a run. Larry Jaster replaced Washburn, and Cash singled in the second run of the inning. Horton came to bat. Northrup kneeled in the on-deck circle.

Jaster had trouble pitching to Horton.

McLain's pitching, and it looks like Willie's getting a walk, thought Northrup as he waited for his turn to hit. *The bases could be loaded when I'm up.*

Horton walked. The Cards left Jaster in because he's a left-hander and Northrup bats left.

Northrup cracked the ball high to right field and it struck concrete in the grandstand and ricocheted into a runway below. The grand slam specialist with four during the season had hit another in the World Series. McLain had his eight runs.

Around the bases Northrup danced and into the mob scene in the dugout.

"Let's simmer down," yelled Mayo Smith at his exuberant athletes. "Don't anybody step on his foot."

The Tigers had six runs in the inning and still there was none out. Ron Willis walked Freehan and hit Don Wert. McLain sacrificed them along, the first out. McAuliffe, up again, was walked intentionally to load the bases. Stanley hit a grounder and forced Freehan at home for the second out.

Then Kaline singled, his second hit in the inning, to drive in two runs. Dick Hughes came in and Cash batted in a run on his second hit and Horton singled in another run.

Finally Northrup flied out for the third out.

The Tigers had scored 10 runs in the third, and McLain returned to the mound with a 12–0 lead. Kaline made it 13–0 with his second home run of the Series and third hit of the game in the fifth.

With two outs in the ninth, McLain gave up the Cardinals' only run.

He had redeemed himself by winning, 13–1, and pitching the Tigers into the seventh game of the World Series.

"I didn't have to prove a Goddamn thing today," said McLain. "I want to thank the players. I wish I could take each of them into salary negotiations with me. Like Northrup. He's hit five grand slams this year, and four of them were while I was pitching."

McLain had received the booing treatment from the people of St. Louis.

"I've been booed before and I've been booed by better fans than these," said McLain. "I've been booed by the best fans in the world in Detroit."

"Everybody felt we'd lost it when we were down, three to one," said Northrup.

"We battled back—this has been the trademark of our team," said Al Kaline, who had 11 hits in the Series. "The big thing is we won the way we'd been winning before. Games you can't lose. Now we've won these games and the Cards have a game they can lose.

"We wanted it to go down to seven games. We didn't want to get beat four games to one. I guess my best quote of the Series was the other day in the rain when I said it was a team effort when we lost."

But still the Tigers knew tomorrow Bob Gibson would be waiting for them, his arm as rested as it could be in October.

"We were down three to one, and we're very happy to be going back against Mr. Gibson," said Mayo Smith. "I'm pitching Mickey Lolich against him tomorrow."

OCTOBER 10

Mickey Lolich, victorious twice in the World Series, stood near the batting cage before today's seventh game.

"Tomorrow I've got to change a gear on a motorcycle," he said. "I've been trying to do that for two weeks."

A newspaperman asked him a simple question.

"How do I feel about pitching against Bob Gibson?" repeated Lolich. "I believe I'll be pitching against eight other guys."

Curt Flood's long lead was short-lived as he ended up being tagged out by Mickey Stanley.

UPI

Denny McLain stood off to one side with the audience gathered around him.

"I'll be in the bullpen today," said the 31-game winner. "Trying to put together a comedy act."

Mayo Smith, the maneuverer, stood arms crossed over the blue DETROIT on his gray traveling uniform. Mickey Stanley would be his shortstop for the seventh straight game.

"It's a tribute to Stanley that you writers don't go around asking questions of him anymore," said Smith.

"When you were down three games to one," asked a writer, "did you talk to any of your players?"

"I talked to Freehan, McAuliffe, Horton and Cash," said Smith. "I'm not a good psychologist. The greatest asset a manager can have is a degree in psychology."

The invincible Bob Gibson towered on the pitching mound. The first ten batters he faced went out in order, five of them on strikeouts. Then Stanley singled with one out in the fourth.

After the Tigers had batted six times, Stanley still was the only base runner they'd had. Entering the Cardinals' sixth, Lolich was almost as excellent as Gibson. Lolich had allowed only two singles.

But in the bottom of the sixth, Lou Brock led off with a single to left, his thirteenth base hit of the World Series. Brock has a trick—he leads 15 feet off first and forces the pitcher to attempt a pickoff there. As the pitcher makes his motion he takes off for second. Brock stole a lot of bases that way. One of his seven steals in the Series had been achieved against Lolich in the second game on this precise tactic.

Now Brock led off by 11, 12, 13, 14 and finally 15 feet. Lolich looked over and threw to Norm Cash. Brock flew toward second. Cash relayed the throw to Stanley at short. Stanley applied the tag. Brock was caught stealing.

With one out, Curt Flood singled. He took his long lead and Lolich threw to Cash. Flood was trapped, and he raced for second. Cash again threw and Flood was tagged in a rundown. Lolich was out of the inning.

Gibson continued his mastery in the seventh. He struck out Stanley and got Al Kaline on a ground ball to third. Two outs.

Cash came up and hit the ball into right field for the second hit off Gibson. Willie Horton followed with a single past shortstop into left.

Gibson now had to get Jim Northrup, the graying outfielder, the Gray Fox to his teammates. Northrup lined the ball to center field.

Curt Flood saw the ball and took a step in. Quickly he turned and stumbled and started running out—faster and faster. And the ball kept slicing—away, away. It whizzed past Flood and landed in the grass and rolled.

As he rounded first base, Northrup looked out and saw Flood still pursuing the elusive ball. Cash scored to break the 0–0 tie and Willie Horton scored and Jim Northrup went into third with his two-run triple.

A moment later Bill Freehan got his second hit of the Series, a double to left out of reach of Brock's dive. The Tigers had three runs off Bob Gibson.

Lolich retired the Cardinals in the seventh and again in the eighth. In the ninth, Horton singled and Northrup singled and then little Don Wert singled. The Tigers had a 4–0 lead and three outs to get.

Flood lined to Ray Oyler, whom Mayo had just stationed at shortstop. Orlando Cepeda popped a foul and Freehan yanked off his catcher's mask and caught the ball. Two outs. Just one more. Lolich pitched and Mike Shannon drove the ball into the left-field seats for a home run. Still one to go.

Tim McCarver took his swing and lifted the ball to the right of home plate. Again Freehan took off his mask and waited for the ball to descend. It plopped into his catcher's mitt, and an instant later Mickey Lolich plopped into Freehan's hugging arms.

Mickey Lolich does the victory leap aboard Bill Freehan.

The Detroit Tigers were champions of the world.

There was a wild celebration at home plate. The Tigers had defeated Bob Gibson in their own way, with a late rally, and won the seventh game, 4–1.

It was 4:06 in the afternoon back in Detroit—and the people came out of the office buildings and factories and kissed and yelled and honked their horns. Paper fluttered from the windows and piled up until the debris was calf-deep and the people had trouble walking through it. And there was so much confetti thrown it lined the embankments of the expressways for 15 miles from downtown.

Thousands of people got into autos and started the 20-mile journey to Metropolitan Airport, bumper to bumper.

And in the visitors' clubhouse in St. Louis the brilliant television lights were turned on and clubhouse man John Hand broke out the champagne.

Off in a corner, away from the main din, Al Kaline, the sixteen-year veteran in his first World Series, stood grinning. The bat Mayo Smith maneuvered into the lineup had hit .379 in the World Series.

"It was worth waiting sixteen years," said Kaline, who had never attended a World Series ball game until eight days ago. "I'd seen my other World Series in the country club, watching on TV. I considered people lucky to be in the Series. I knew all along I'd get into the Series someday, maybe as a pinch hitter.

"I never expected to have this good a Series. I was one of the lucky ones."

Kaline held his own bottle of champagne around the neck. Occasionally he sipped from it, sometimes sharing it with others.

"Gibson is the greatest pitcher I've ever faced. To beat him and win the World Series all in one game is really great. We just wanted to get into the seventh game real bad—for our pride after the way we played the first two games in Detroit.

"Our team made a great comeback. We were embarrassed the way we played. If we got beat, we wanted to get beat by Gibson because he's the best.

"We bounced back all year like this. We just got a bunch of hits together in this game, just like we did all year in the seventh, eighth and ninth innings. The big secret to this club in the late innings is everybody just goes for base hits, they stop trying for the long ball."

As Kaline talked softly, there was bedlam in the center of the room. Denny McLain grabbed a bottle of champagne and shook it and streamed the charged-up liquid at the sports writers, at the TV cameras, at his teammates.

"Who's number one in the whole world?" yelled Earl Wilson. "We are. We're the greatest team in the world."

And in the manager's room Mayo Smith stood at the desk, on which there were three bottles of champagne.

"The turning point of the Series," Mayo said for the fifteenth time, "had to be the play on Brock in the fifth game. The play at the plate. Freehan caused this by his position at the plate. I'd have to say this was the determining factor. Horton got rid of the ball right away. He made a helluva throw.

"That play let us come from where we were to where we are now."

"I think the whole damn World Series was Mickey Stanley playing shortstop," said Norm Cash, who had led the Tigers in hitting with a .385 average. "Without him playing shortstop, Al wouldn't have been in the Series."

And finally the noise diminished and everyone went to the showers to wash off the champagne. Dick McAuliffe took his with Jim Campbell's lucky yellow sun hat on his head.

The Tigers got aboard their airplane to fly back to Detroit and were informed they would be unable to land at Metro. There were 35,000 people out there waiting, and they had broken down the barriers and were running down the runways. Fragmented glass littered the landing strips.

In a joyous display of the championship trophy are, left to right, Dick McAuliffe, Jim Northrup and Mickey Stanley.

The chartered plane carrying the World Champions was diverted to Willow Run Airport, some 15 miles from Metro.

On the airplane Mickey Lolich, the twelfth pitcher to win three games in a World Series, only recently liberated from the bullpen, talked to columnist Pete Waldmeir.

"I guess I'm an unlikely hero," said Lolich. "Potbelly, big ears . . . just a steady guy who shows up every day and gets the job done as best he knows how.

"There's always somebody else making a big deal out of things, getting the ink, making the moves. But you know what? I knew all along I could do it. And I'm so thrilled

Detroit Tigers

The champs:

Front row: Don Wert, John Wyatt, Tony Cuccinello, Wally Moses, Mayo Smith, Hal Naragon, John Sain, Wayne Comer, Willie Horton, Mickey Lolich.

Second row: John Hand (equipment), Bill Behm (trainer), Julio Moreno (batting practice pitcher), Jim Northrup, Ray Oyler, Earl Wilson, Fred Lasher, Don McMahon, Al Kaline, Charles C. Creedon (traveling secretary).

rd row: **Dick Tracewski, Norm Cash, Ed Mathews, Jim Price, Jon Warden, Denny McLain, Gates Brown, John Hiller, Dick McAuliffe.**

ck row: **Roy Face, Bob Christian, Mickey Stanley, Joe Sparma, Daryl Patterson, Pat Dobson, Tom Matchick, Bill Freehan.**

that all those people are down there waiting for us. It's the biggest day of my life.

"A dream. It's like a dream. Everything's going to happen fast for the next few days, and I don't want anything to spoil it. I'm not going to ask for a hundred thousand dollars. I'd settle for half that. I don't want to be a fast-buck guy."

And the airplane landed and the throng that found out it had been diverted welcomed the World Champions.

Downtown 150,000 people jammed the streets . . . store windows were broken . . . crime and arrests occurred. But mostly there were people throwing paper and getting drunk.

The lights on the gas company sign overlooking the Lodge Expressway near the ball park exit flashed a brand new message:

HAIL TO THE CHAMPS

EPILOGUE—DECEMBER 1

Denny McLain, the 31-game-winning organist, put on his white mink coat worth $1,500 and walked out to his opening in the Riviera Hotel in Las Vegas.

"I wouldn't trade a dozen Mickey Loliches for one Bob Gibson," McLain told his audience.

He soon realized what he'd said, and the next night he tried to say what he really meant.

"I wouldn't trade a dozen Mickey Loliches for one Bob Gibson," said McLain. The comment made the wire services, and McLain tried again the third night.

"I wouldn't trade a dozen Bob Gibsons for one Mickey Lolich," he said. "That's what I meant to say."

McLain appeared on the Ed Sullivan show and Mickey Lolich was in the audience.

Lolich became a singer and went to Las Vegas with a Detroit combo. He appeared on the *Joey Bishop Show*.

Mayo Smith was roasted by the Saints and Sinners in New York and had a comment.

"Mickey Stanley will be my center fielder next year," said the maneuverer.

McLain traveled from one booking to another and went in to talk 1969 contract with Jim Campbell. He signed quickly. His contract was short of $100,000—estimated at $65,000 to $70,000.

The postseason awards were announced.

McLain was picked unanimously as the Cy Young Award winner as the American League's best pitcher.

He was named the league's Most Valuable Player in another unanimous vote.

Mayo Smith was selected as the Manager of the Year. Jim Campbell was baseball's Executive of the Year.

One afternoon Denny McLain complained of stomach pains while in Campbell's office. McLain was rushed to the hospital for an emergency appendectomy.

And Mickey Lolich was called to duty with the Air National Guard. But for winning three games in the World Series, Lolich was given one year's grace from KP.

The Year of the Tiger brought all kinds of rewards.